MR. LINCOLN'S CITY

MR. LINCOLN'S CITY

An Illustrated Guide
to the Civil War Sites of Washington

Richard M. Lee

EPM Publications, Inc.
McLean, Virginia

Library of Congress Cataloging in Publication Data

Lee, Richard M. (Richard McGowan)
    Mr. Lincoln's city.

    Bibliography: p.
    1. Washington (D.C.)—Description—1951–   —Guide-
books. 2. Historic sites—Washington (D.C.)—Guide-
books. 3. Washington (D.C.)—History—Civil War, 1861–
1865. I. Title. II. Title: Civil War sites of Washington.
F192.3.L44   917.53′044   81-3267
ISBN 0-914440-48-9   AACR2

Book Design by Tom Huestis

TABLE OF CONTENTS

This note was found in the fly leaf of a book near General Early's headquarters at Blair House, Silver Spring, Maryland.

Near Washington
July 12, 1864

Now Uncle Abe, you had better be quiet the balance of your Administration, as we came near your town this time to show you what we could do. But if you go on in your mad career, we will come again soon, and then you had better stand from under.

Yours Respectfully, the worst rebel you ever saw,
Fifty-eighth Virginia Infantry

PART I

Washington in Wartime, 1861–1865

MAP 1.

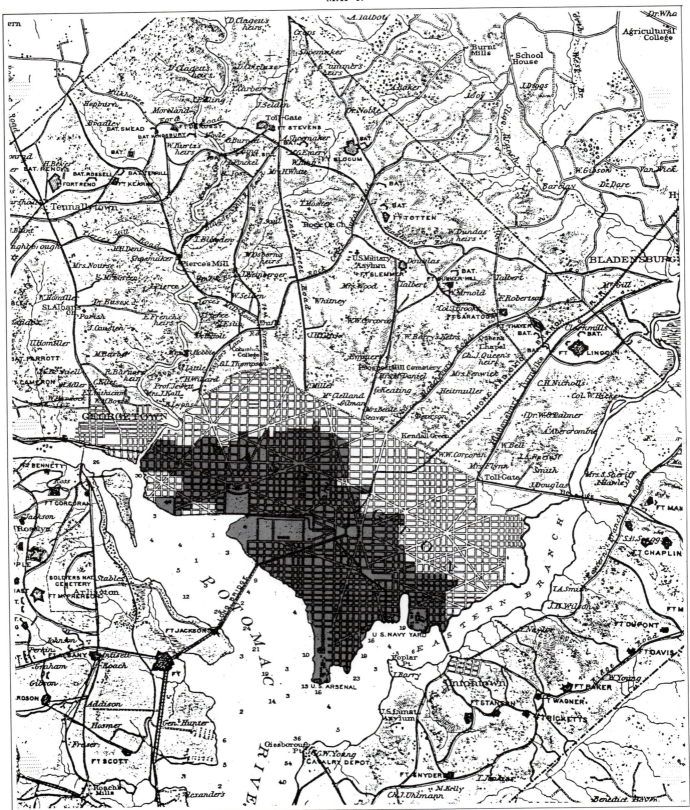

Washington During the Civil War, 1861–1865. The city shown here is from the early 19th Century plan. Washington didn't reach these limits until the 1890's. Its smaller size during the war is shown by the shaded area.

Washington in Wartime, 1861–1865

In April of 1861 the nation's capital was a bare start on the grand design of the founding fathers. Though the setting among the wooded hills and wide panoramas of the Potomac River Valley was majestic, the city of shabby brick and wooden buildings scattered along dirty streets presented, at best, an unfinished appearance.

The elevation was low—on the banks of the tidal Potomac with its swamps and stagnant surface waters. Floods sometimes swept over lower Pennsylvania Avenue. During the scorching, humid summers, flies and mosquitoes were everywhere, and the primitive sanitation of the times made the city a malodorous, unhealthy place. Much of the drinking water came from contaminated local wells. Family privies were in general use; hotel flush toilets emptied into back lots, the City Canal or Tiber Creek.

Typhoid, tuberculosis, malaria and dysentery took their annual toll. Epidemics had been part of the city's past, even the dreaded Asiatic cholera. Diplomats from Europe considered Washington a hardship post and left their families at home. When a member of the British Foreign Service reported that he was "climate proof," his senior responded, "He is the man for Washington."

This unhurried, untidy southern town, made up mostly of Virginia and Maryland families, government clerks, politicians and those who housed, fed and served them—where goats, pigs and cows wandered freely through streets and vacant lots—suddenly, in May 1861 found itself the war center of an aroused North. Its nearly 63,000 souls were catapulted into a world of action and violence, crowds of strangers and an atmosphere of political and military crisis.

bringing the Union Army to battle at a time and place of his choosing. Catching them off guard, scattered or on bad ground, he might reverse the odds of greater numbers and destroy the blue force. Washington, the prize, would then lie open.

Brady photo of the man who kept Washington in fear and uncertainty for most of the war. General Robert E. Lee as he appeared in Richmond just after the surrender at Appomattox.

National Archives

The Real and Present Danger

Southern leaders were determined to capture Washington from the start. Its seizure meant independence for the Confederacy. But their great commander, Robert E. Lee, knew that first he had to destroy the Union Army of the Potomac which stood in great numbers between him and the city. His campaigns suggest that he recognized and used the relationship between the city and the defending Union Army. When Confederate forces threatened Washington, as they did several times, the Lincoln Administration could be counted on to react with alarm; frantic orders would go out for the Army to drive the Rebels off. Herein lay Lee's opportunity for

Geographic constraints as well as Union naval control of the Potomac and Chesapeake waters restricted General Lee's Army to an approach to Washington by one of two routes (Map 2). His columns could move north through the central Virginia Piedmont and occupy the Centreville-Bull Run area, a day's march from Washington. The Union Army, in reaction to Washington pressure, could be counted on to gather and give battle. The South won three battles on this ground, but failed to destroy the Blue Army; it escaped to the safety of Washington's forts.

As a variant and an even greater threat, General Lee could and did lead his Army north of Bull Run, across the Potomac River at Leesburg, to seize Frederick, Maryland. Here he threatened Washington from its weakest side, the north. Again he could count on an alarmed Yankee Army pursuing and attacking him as soon as possible. This happened at Antietam (September 1862) where bad luck helped ruin his plans.

General Lee's second approach (Map 2) was a march west over the Blue Ridge Mountains into the Valley of Virginia. In June 1863 he moved his army down this valley and appeared north of the Potomac River in Maryland. Here he was poised to attack southeastwards toward Washington, precisely as one of his generals actually did in July 1864, entering the District itself. Washington was barely saved by the last-minute arrival of two Union Army corps from General Grant's force at Petersburg.

A further option of this approach was for General Lee to invade central Pennsylvania. This he did in mid-1863, not to seize and hold this farming region, but to entice the Union Army into the open under conditions that would enable him to destroy it. However, the absence of General Stuart's cavalry at a critical time, the eyes and ears of the Southern Army, combined with the rapid advance of the Union force, caused Lee's Army to grope prematurely into battle with the Federal Army. The advantages of high ground and good defensive position lay with the North. The South lost the hard fought three-day battle at Gettysburg, the beginning of the end for the Confederacy.

The threatening presence of the Confederate Army, moving variously south, west and north of Washington, was an unnerving influence on the city's daily life for four long years. From time to time loyal citizens, including the President and his Cabinet, felt themselves in the gravest peril. This sense of danger accounts for the rapid construction, mostly during the winter of 1861–62, of a thirty-seven-mile ring of sixty-eight forts surrounding the city. By the end of the fighting in 1865 these forts were the military marvel of their time—an elaborate, mutually supporting system containing over 800 heavy fortress cannon. Connecting the forts were twenty miles of trenches for infantry troops interspersed with ninety-three prepared artillery positions to be manned if needed. (See Appendix, "A Ring of Forts")

Washington—The Arsenal of the North

The city's location was paradoxical. On the northern border of Virginia, it sat just 100 miles from the heart of Confederate power at Richmond. Never feeling truly secure, Washington nevertheless grew, behind its forts, into the most powerful base the Union had (Map 3).

Hardly had war begun when camps, warehouses, depots, immense stacks of ammunition, food, equipment and long rows of cannon, caissons, wagons and ambulances began sprouting up all over town in vacant lots and open spaces. Centers of activity included the Navy Yard, the Army Arsenal (now Fort McNair), and the Potomac wharves at Sixth and Seventh Streets SW. By 1863 another hub of activity had grown along the Maryland Avenue railroad yards. These busy centers lined the southern rim of the city fronting on the Anacostia and Potomac Rivers.

On the capital's western limits arose the city's largest accumulation of supplies, storehouses and barracks in a vacant area still called Foggy Bottom. Beginning about Nineteenth Street it led westward toward the Western wharves at the Potomac end of G Street. A large Army camp south of Washington Circle, a huge remount depot holding up to 30,000 horses and mules, harness repair and blacksmith shops, forage dumps,

MAP 2.

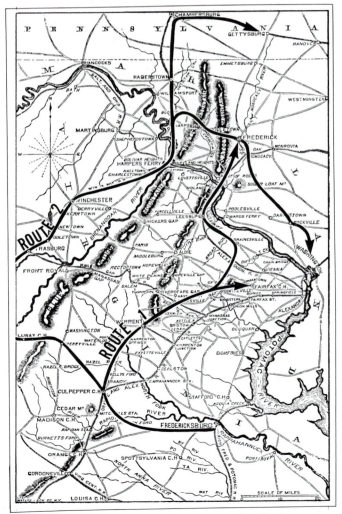

Confederate Approaches to Washington and the North.
ROUTE 1 – *The Piedmont Route*   **ROUTE 2** – *The Valley Route*

MAP 3.

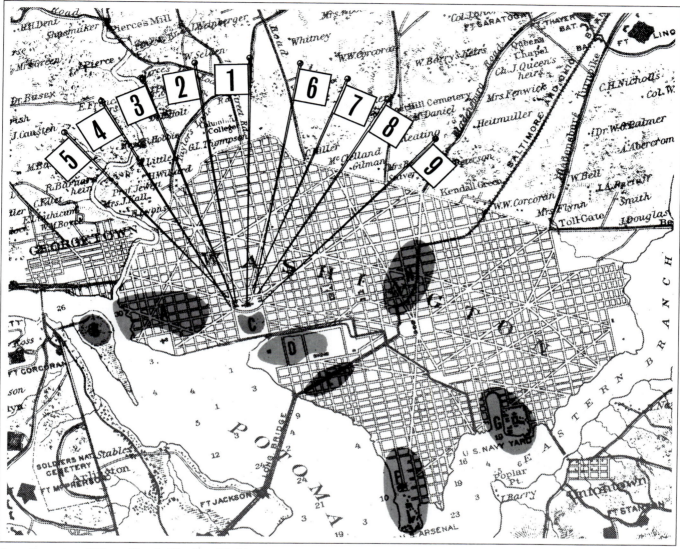

Some Important Military Sites in Wartime Washington.
Top Union headquarters and offices:

Flag 1 – Commander-in-Chief's office, the White House.
Flag 2 – War Department, SE corner 17th Street and Pennsylvania Avenue.
Flag 3 – Navy Department, east side corner 17th and F Streets.
Flag 4 – Union Army Headquarters, the Winder building, NW corner 17th and F Streets.
Flag 5 – Adjutant General's Offices, NW corner of 17th Street and Pennsylvania Avenue.
Flag 6 – Headquarters Defenses of Washington, NE corner Pennsylvania Avenue and Madison Place.
Flag 7 – Headquarters Army of the Potomac (Fall–Winter '61–'62), SE corner H Street and Madison Place.
Flag 8 – Surgeon General's Office, NW corner of 15th Street and Pennsylvania Avenue, second floor Riggs Bank building.
Flag 9 – Paymaster General's Office, SE corner 15th and F Streets, Old Corcoran building.

Wartime Army and Navy repair, supply, training and other centers in the city.

Area A – Foggy Bottom–Western Wharves supply complex.
Area B – Analostin Island camp and training area.
Area C – White Lot (Ellipse) army bivouac and hospital sites.
Area D – Washington Monument/Mall slaughter house and grazing grounds, also army bivouac, training and testing grounds for new weapons, etc.
Area E – Maryland Avenue depot, rail yards and storehouses.
Area F – U.S. Arsenal, largest in the Union (now Fort McNair).
Area G – Navy Yard with repair facilities, naval supplies and ordnance for warships.
Area H – B. and O. rail depot and repair yards with its Soldier's Rest, camps and supply areas centered roughly near present Union Station.

Rows of field artillery pieces at Washington Arsenal (now Fort McNair) awaiting shipment to the front in Virginia.

Library of Congress

bordering Tiber Creek. It gathered around the Baltimore and Ohio railroad depot and repair yards, the city's lifeline to the North. Here also lay an unsightly mix of army camps, a mess hall and barracks for transient troops, a block of saloons along New Jersey Avenue and the shanty town of Swampoodle.

Near the downtown area the Washington Monument grounds did wartime duty as a large army slaughterhouse. Thousands of doomed cattle grazed close by on the mall. The combined smells of offal, the nearby city dump and the city canal were nauseating. A block west of the White House, a brand new Art Gallery built by the banker, Mr. W. W. Corcoran, turned overnight into the Army's Depot of Clothing and Equippage that poured out hundreds of cases of clothing a day.

camps for wagon trains, mess halls, a large bakery and commissary warehouses filled the grounds now occupied by the State Department, the Kennedy Center, part of the Watergate Apartments and most of George Washington University.

A few blocks from the Capitol and along the northern fringes of the city another untidy conglomeration of supply buildings and yards collected on the wastelands

These were but a few of the more important places. Camps sprang up all over town. Citizens never ceased to be alarmed at the Army's appetite for more and more space. Wherever one looked there were tents, white washed frame buildings, barracks and army wagons. It took 10,000 soldiers and civilians to operate this Washington base; their sole job was to push the "beans and bullets" by road, rail and water to the Army in Virginia.

Even more important to the war effort was a number

The Foggy Bottom–Western Wharves supply complex. Notice Washington Circle in the foreground, then Camp Fry on both sides of Twenty-third Street. In the right background are the warehouses grouped near the Western Wharves at the terminus of G Street. In the left background are the support buildings and open spaces of Camp Fuller (1861–1863), a giant remount depot and camps for wagon trains.

Library of Congress

of small buildings and houses in a half-circle close around the north, east and west sides of the White House serving as headquarters and offices (Map 3). There was no Union Pentagon—just a group of scattered, modest places where the Northern war effort was hammered out; in those days orders went by telegraph to the forces on land and sea. Never one for waiting for his officers to come to him, Mr. Lincoln was forever walking to and from these offices, night and day, to do business with his war leaders and generals.

Richmond. One Army advanced up the Valley route toward Lynchburg and was stopped cold. Another, under General Butler, advanced toward Richmond along the south bank of the James River with the same result. The main effort, made up of Grant's Army of 118,000 men, pounded away from the north, and then curled around to the south to finally take Richmond from the rear.

At first he supplied this large force from Washington, using the Orange and Alexandria Railroad which followed the Piedmont route from Washington (Map 4). Then, during the Battle of Spotsylvania, he switched to

The Western Wharves from the Potomac. Georgetown is to the left. Where one sees the group of low warehouses to the right now rises the Kennedy Center. The Wharf was about where the southern portion of the Watergate Apartments face west toward the river. *Library of Congress*

Washington—Hub of Attack into Virginia

Four great routes led into the Virginia heartland from the city, two more than General Lee had for approaching Washington (Map 4). Of course, Union armies could and did use the same two routes that Lee used, the Piedmont and Valley routes, marching south instead of north. Union naval control of the Potomac and Chesapeake Bay provided the Federals with two more. One was by river down the Potomac to Acquia Creek, then by land to nearby Fredericksburg—the shortest route of all toward Richmond. The other also used the Potomac River, and thence the Chesapeake Bay to the York and James Rivers. The Union used both water routes to move vast tonnages of supplies and entire armies safely into the center of Virginia.

General Grant wove all these routes into his plans for the campaign begun in May 1864 which finally captured

Brady photograph of General Grant at his field headquarters near Cold Harbor, June, 1864. Here he lost 12,000 men, but it was part of his strategy of relentless pressure that won the war ten months later. *National Archives*

the Aquia Creek route, resupplying his army and evacuating many thousands of wounded, mostly to Washington hospitals. Again, General Grant struck hard at Cold Harbor, near Richmond, this time receiving supplies and fresh troops through the York River base at White House. Stopped again by Lee, the Blue Army shifted south of Richmond to attack the city's main rail center at Petersburg. Closing the White House base, Grant opened an enormous new supply point on the James River at City Point. By the flexible, skillfully combined use of all the approaches available to him from Washington, General Grant was able to maintain a relentless and overwhelming pressure on the hungry, weakening Confederate Army in the trenches around Richmond.

MAP 4.

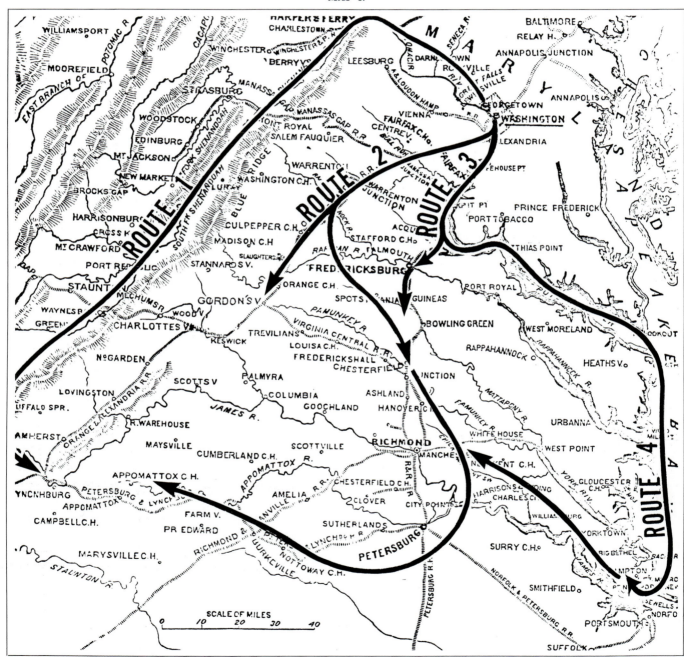

Union Approaches into Virginia.
ROUTE 1 – The Valley Route
ROUTE 2 – The Piedmont Route
ROUTE 3 – Potomac–Acquia Creek Route
ROUTE 4 – Potomac–Chesapeake Route

The People of the Wartime City

While all this fighting was going on, surprising changes were taking place in Washington. From its pre-war population of not quite 63,000 souls, the city literally exploded to a population which at times exceeded 200,000 people. People flocked to take advantage of the opportunities for profit, service and power which the war created in Washington, with the result that the civilian population at least doubled. Then there was the soldier population. The men who manned the forts, patrols, checkpoints and guard posts provided a garrison which fluctuated from 30,000 men to sometimes many more and sometimes far fewer. The work force of the supply base numbered about 10,000, and at any one time from 15,000 to over 50,000 sick and wounded soldiers lay in the hospitals and convalescent camps spread from Alexandria to the hills north of Washington.

Moving to and from the fighting in Virginia were sometimes large numbers of troops, sometimes almost none at all. During the first winter of the war, the whole Army of the Potomac, by spring over 200,000 men, camped around Washington. After the lost Second Battle of Bull Run, possibly 140,000 men gathered to hold the city in that dark hour. To residents of old Washington the city must have seemed a foreign, unreal place with its floating population of strangers.

At the top of the social ladder were two small elite groups. Most of the tiny band of white aristocracy, southern in tradition and blood, were devoted to the Confederacy, and some had sons fighting with Lee. They were suspect, but lived quietly and kept a guarded tongue. Those who didn't, at times as many as 300 Washington and Georgetown citizens, found themselves in cells in the Old Capitol or some other military prison. The plight of these once important people was sad. Excluded from official life and society, often financially burdened and grieved by the loss of loved ones and friends in battle, their influence ended abruptly with the arrival of Mr. Lincoln and his Republican supporters in early 1861.

In the mansions along H Street, and elsewhere in the city's northwest quarter, lived a small ruling class of Union political leaders, wealthy businessmen and senior military officers with their families. These men were mostly selfmade, contentious and forceful leaders. Their manners generally lacked the polish and civility of the displaced southerners. Money, position and political power were entrees here. Their social season began with the new year and was suspended during hot weather. It featured a procession of receptions, diplomatic and other balls, dinners and theater parties. Lack-

An everyday sight—a crowd of talking, gesturing men gathered in the lobby of Willard's Hotel.

White House Collection

ing an aristocratic background, the new elite relied more on display—mansions, fine clothes, furniture and carriages. Impressed by titles, they gave much attention to foreign nobility and such home-grown titles as Senator and General. Wives too enjoyed their own titles, as in Mrs. Judge so-and-so.

Social life flourished at the hotels, especially the Willard, where the well-dressed, affluent and influential gathered at the restaurants, reception rooms and bars. The women presided on the second floor where periodic hops (dances) were held.

As the war moved toward its bloody climax in 1864, and the city overflowed with the horror of far too many sick, wounded and dying men, an epidemic of gaiety, extravagance and party-going infected society. Perhaps it was a reaction to so much tragedy. On their way to

one festivity or another the carriages of the rich and pleasure bound mingled in the streets with seemingly unnoticed lines of muddy ambulances drawn by plodding horses toward the hospitals.

Excluded from the social life of the two elites a large, hard-working middle class went about its daily business in the city. Among them were the middle and lower levels of the clerks whose ranks, rising from 1500 in 1861 to over 7000 in 1865, had to cope with the mushrooming workload of war. They received small salaries, lived in crowded rooming houses and ate their meals at common tables. Even in good times clerks barely made ends meet; their families generally lived away from the expensive capital. With a wartime inflation gripping the country, wages drifted behind prices; in 1864 retail prices rose 76% over those in 1861 and the cost of room and board rose by 150%. Clerks were hard pressed but the job they did before the day of typewriters and telephones was an essential one. According to a popular saying, "the flying fingers of thousands of clerks did all the business of government."

The bulk of the middle class provided some kind of service to the government, its officials, the citizens and the strangers arriving and departing the city. They were shop keepers and inn keepers, middle managers, professionals in law and medicine, and especially businessmen. As a whole they were shrewd, upwardly mobile and supporters of the Union. Taking advantage of the wartime economic boom, many did well and some laid the foundations of banking and business fortunes. By the war's end they were becoming entrenched as Washington's permanent establishment for, unlike the politicians and the military, they were not transients. In time they became the backbone of its churches, the inheritors of its economic future and those who watched over the growth of the physical city.

At the bottom of the social scale were the laborers, many of them immigrants, and thousands of newly-arrived former slaves. For them life was a grim and chancey business; the city had far more laborers than it could employ. To keep solvent a number fell into careers of crime and a host of other doubtful activities. Some women developed devices for tying illegal whiskey bottles under their long skirts, and then walked out to the camps to sell their wares to the soldiers.

Living among the lower class was a teeming population from northern cities of gamblers, hucksters, prostitutes, conmen, pickpockets and the like. Small groups dismounted from the trains daily with their carpetbags, hopeful of finding easy marks among the newcomers to the city. Numbers of smooth-talking, well-dressed men and women worked confidence games along Pennsylvania Avenue, attempting to bilk the unwary. South of the Avenue, and in other notorious haunts, the business of vice and crime, in one form or another, went on behind the backs of the police and military patrols.

Then as now, the most noticeable people in town were visitors. They flooded in from the North searching

The social scene—a grand ball at Willard's.

The Junior League of Washington

for influence, position, profit, a cause to serve, or perhaps a loved one in a hospital. Louisa May Alcott, author of *Little Women,* served as a nurse in the Union Hotel Hospital in Georgetown. Walt Whitman was captured by the sheer drama of the wartime city and stayed to devote himself to the wounded. The doctor-poet, Oliver Wendell Holmes, came down from Boston to find his son who had been wounded at Antietam—a son later to become a great Supreme Court justice. Clara Barton, a shy Patent Office clerk from Massachusetts, forgot her diffidence and followed the army fearlessly into the battlefields to help the wounded, returning at brief intervals to her rooms on Seventh Street. Some, like Jay Cooke, came to make money, and did. Inventors promoted their ideas in offices around the city, creating a rich harvest of weapons of destruction. All kinds of people crowded into the shabby city and the miracle is, it somehow absorbed them.

Miss Louisa Buckner being searched (November, 1862) at the Provost Marshall's headquarters at Nineteenth and I Streets. She was caught trying to carry quinine through the lines to a Confederacy hard pressed for medicines. Her stay at the Old Capitol Prison was short, for she was the niece of the Postmaster General.

Martin Luther King Library

Washington— The City of the Wounded

In May of 1861, as the war was getting under way, the only hospital in Washington was a dispensary on Judiciary Square. Fourteen months and several bloody campaigns later, in October of 1862, nearly sixty hospitals were spread from Georgetown across Washington to the hills north of the city. In addition, there were nineteen others in and around Alexandria, five miles to the south.

How had all this come about? The city's proximity to the fighting, and the fact that it lay at the hub of the routes from the Virginia battlefields (the roads, railroads and the Potomac River), made it the natural receiving point for wounded men. This was not well understood at first by the medical authorities whose efforts the first year of the war could be classed as too little and too late. Frustration impelled improvisation.

When the sick and wounded of General McClellan's Peninsular battles arrived by the boatload at the Sixth Street wharves in spring, 1862, the army had no choice but to commandeer hotels, churches, fraternal halls, schools and colleges, public buildings, private homes and even the insane asylum. In the wake of the Second Battle of Bull Run in late August, thousands more wounded and exhausted men were cast up on the city's doorstep, even the Capitol of the United States became a hospital. Three weeks later another dreadful inundation of torn and broken bodies descended from Western Maryland, the harvest of the fierce fighting at South Mountain and Antietam. During the last four months of

1862 the number of wounded pouring into the city rose like a ghastly fever chart until more than 56,000 men were undergoing hospital treatment in the city. By this time thousands of less severely wounded men were being shipped by rail to hospitals in other eastern cities; Washington could not accomodate them all.

By early 1863 a change for the better became noticeable. The makeshift hospitals began to close down, their patients moving to larger and sometimes specially designed hospitals. The best were built in the new pavilion style—a number of low, shed-like white frame buildings, each one a ward connected by covered passageways to other wards and administrative buildings. They reflected the medical passion of the age for "pure air" as the preferred way to reduce "hospital poisons", thought to collect amidst concentrations of patients. A pavilion hospital generally had ten or eleven wards and a few administrative buildings; each ward held fifty or so cots. Holding about 600 patients, it could quickly expand into tents or nearby buildings.

Louisa May Alcott tells of the ambulances' arrival outside a Washington hospital. The weather was dark and bitter cold in December 1862 when frozen and shattered men arrived after the defeat at Fredericksburg. First the begrimed soldiers had to be washed before being put to bed. She picked her first patient, a small Irishman, and they were soon laughing as she plied her washrag.

Walt Whitman's letters also give us the flavor of life in the hospitals. He saw women working in the wards, in numbers, for the first time in American history. Among them were the nuns of the Sisters of Charity and black contract nurses. The work load was heavy, and some gave up in the face of many doctors' hostility toward them and their dread of witnessing so much suffering and death in the wards. Others, like Miss Alcott, fell seriously ill and had to leave. But many stayed for the war's duration. Whitman thought the older women who had been mothers made the best nurses. They sensed better what to do and say, for their patients were hardly more than boys. These devoted women brought qualities of gentleness and caring to the sick, badly needed in the grim hospitals of that time.

The wards had a constant flow of visitors. Many were nuisances, harrassing the sick with Victorian sermonizing, interrupting needed rest, picking favorites or gossiping incessantly. The best tonic for the men was a visit from their families. All over the Union fathers, mothers and wives—sometimes whole families—got on trains and descended upon Washington. They hunted patiently through the maze of hospitals, or badgered the bureaucracy, until they found their loved one. In many cases mothers and wives nursed their own wounded. Heartbreak was in store for many a woman trying to hold back a soldier slipping slowly toward death.

From time to time, with a touch of awe, these Americans from distant and often humble places would see the lanky figure of the President going slowly from bed to bed, touching a shoulder here, an arm there, the hand of somebody's stricken son. "God bless you," he'd say and pause a moment.

In his memoirs, Dr. John Brinton recalled a difficult operation at Armory Square Hospital during which he removed a man's arm at the shoulder. At the end of the

The kind of hospital used when the wounded started pouring into Washington in the Spring of 1862—any place available. This was Trinity Church at Third and C Streets NW.
Library of Congress

The beginning of suitable general hospitals. Mount Pleasant Hospital (March, 1862–August, 1865) was a rebuilt army barracks about one mile north of Florida Avenue on the east side of Fourteenth Street NW. Notice the buildings are all connected and nearby tents are available to accommodate the overflow of wounded men.
Library of Congress

surgery an assisting surgeon congratulated Dr. Brinton on his skill. Then from behind them came a solemn, troubled voice asking, "But what about the soldier?" Startled, Dr. Brinton turned and saw the President.

After times of heavy fighting, as many as fifty soldiers a day died in the city's hospitals. They were placed in pine coffins, taken by ambulance to the cemetery and buried, all at a contract price of $4.99 per soldier. Scandals sometimes occurred because people became calloused to such wholesale death. On one occasion *The Evening Star* blasted Judiciary Square Hospital for leaving a soldier's body naked and exposed for hours on a vacant lot behind the hospital where children played. When Soldier's Home Cemetery became full early in 1864, the dead were taken across the Long Bridge to a new resting place on the Lee's Arlington Estate.

By mid-1863 the number of hospitals in Washington and Georgetown had fallen to about thirty. The new larger hospitals had taken over the greater portion of the patient load, and many wounded were shipped on from Washington, or directly from the battlefields, to new hospitals in other eastern cities, a large number going to Philadelphia and New York. The final great surge of patients came in the spring of 1864 during General Grant's costly, sustained fighting in the battles for Richmond. These heavy attacks produced more than 38,000 Union wounded men in one month's fighting. Though some arrived at Washington in a terrible and neglected condition, the system of

new, large and clean hospitals was far better prepared to treat them. By December 1864 the number of hospitals in the city had fallen to nineteen, but the number of hospitals in the Union continued to climb to meet the overall need.

The end of the war brought a time for evaluation. In spite of a chaotic beginning, the country discovered that its medical care to its soldiers had ended up as a major achievement. Over a million men had passed through the general hospitals with a mortality of only about eight percent, the lowest ever recorded for military hospitals anywhere in the world up to that time. Also, something like a miracle was beginning to happen to American medicine; sobered by its abysmal state at the outbreak of war, the best American doctors began a serious new look at medical science and practice. The pace of the research then begun has continued and accelerated to this day, with wholesale benefits to mankind far beyond the imagination of the Civil War doctor.

By October, 1865, white hospital buildings were coming down all over Washington; only five hospitals remained. Kalorama, last vestige of the city of war hospitals, closed in July, 1867. The only evidence today of the enormous suffering and death Washingtonians witnessed so vividly during those war years are the ranked rows of thousands of tombstones at Soldier's Home and Arlington National Cemeteries.

The Agony of Freedom

On August 14, 1861 the USS Resolute of the Potomac Flotilla, weary from patrolling the Confederate batteries along the west Potomac shores below Washington, dropped anchor off the Navy Yard. Aboard was a small vanguard of the 40,000 blacks who poured into the city during the war years. From Carroll County, Maryland they came—twelve men, three women and two children. What to do with them? It took Secretary of the Navy, Gideon Welles, finally to declare, "Let them go!"

But these people were escaped slaves. The Fugitive Slave Act was still in effect. Routinely police and slave catchers in the city pursued, caught and returned runaway slaves to their Virginia and Maryland masters for a reward. Still the blacks persisted in coming, crossing the Potomac bridges in small groups every day. In the banners of the Union and the blue-clad men who bore them, the slaves sensed their hour of deliverance. Mostly field hands, they arrived in rags and tatters and they came rejoicing—some singing majestic spirituals, and some songs of freedom of their own making.

I ain't goin' to get whipped no more,
I got my ticket
Leavin' th' thicket
An' I'm headin' fo' t' golden shore!

Turmoil over policy continued for nearly a year and a half after the war started. As more blacks arrived Washington police and slave catchers expedited their search for runaway slaves. Conversely, some Army regiments hid blacks in their camps in defiance of civil authorities. Other soldiers surrendered escaped slaves to their masters. General James Wadsworth, the city's military governor, shielded runaway slaves with his provost marshal patrols, and gathered some 400 destitute and sick blacks into a group of houses known as Duff Green's Row at the present location of the Folger Library. Here he housed, fed and protected them. Most of the new arrivals had no place to go and no means of supporting themselves. They crowded into the city's slums as well as the shanty towns near the forts. In time the new freedom became the cruelest of disappointments.

The tide was slowly turning against slavery, however. By April, 1862, Congress had freed the slaves of District residents. A few months later, during the intense anxiety that gripped Washington before the Union victory at Antietam, the President told the Cabinet that "he had made a vow, a covenant, that if God gave us (the Union) the victory in the approaching battle, he would consider it an indication of the Divine will, and that it was his duty to move forward in the cause of emancipation." (Welles, *Diary*) Five days after the battle (September 22, 1862) he issued a preliminary Emancipation Proclamation. It provided that on January 1, 1863, the slaves of masters in rebellion against the United States would be freed.

The months of war passed, and people became aware that its nature was changing. While still very much a crusade to preserve the Union, it was also becoming a war to abolish slavery. As the most interested parties, the blacks on Maryland and Virginia plantations quickly grasped this essential point, and the waves of slaves

An escaped slave in the Union Army. *The Library of Congress*

walking into Washington swelled to a flood. About 10,000 blacks had reached the city by early 1863; the remaining two years saw the arrival of nearly 30,000 more.

There was no national precedent in welfare assistance to care for so many in dire need. The city government had neither funds nor inclination to do much. Private enterprise, survival of the fittest in the spirit of the economic Darwinism of those times, regarded poverty as the deserved and natural fate of those who fell behind in the race for money and security. Private charities, Freedmen societies and concerned individuals did what they could. In his walks near the White House Mr. Lincoln, who didn't carry much money, wrote personal checks to some of these unfortunates. Still in the files of Riggs Bank are his checks "To the colored man with one leg," "To Mr. Johns," and the like.

Utilizing the larger resources of the Army, General Wadsworth established a headquarters for blacks at Twelfth and O Streets NW to register, feed and secure

As Union forces moved south in Virginia, slaves deserted the plantations and started for Washington any way they could.

The Junior League of Washington

River on the southeast slopes of the Lee's Arlington Estate. About 3000 former slaves lived there, cultivating the farms between Fort Corcoran (now Rosslyn) and the Long Bridge (now the Fourteenth Street Bridge). This camp was regarded as a model village, and important tourists, like the Marquis de Chambrun, visited it. The frame buildings were clustered about a central green; workshops were active from morning until dusk; here blacks learned carpentry, tailoring, blacksmithing, cobbling and other trades.

These blacks were spared the abysmal city living conditions endured by the great majority of former slaves, which could hardly have been worse. One visitor to the Murder Bay slum wrote:

> I have visited the Freedmen in their cabins; their sufferings are most heart-rending. The weather is cold, and they have little or no wood. Snow covers the ground; and they have a scanty supply of rags called clothes. The hospital is crowded with the sick. Government gives them a very, very small allowance of soup. Many will die. . . . (*National Freedman,* March 1865)

By the middle of 1863 the need for more soldiers overcame the aversion of many whites to former slaves entering the Union Army. Washington did its share. Two black companies, then a whole regiment, were recruited and trained at a camp on Analostin Island (Roosevelt Island), just across the Potomac channel from Georgetown. Apparently the camp's location was not well known. Even the President and Mrs. Lincoln were said to have wandered about the city in their carriage looking for it. Walt Whitman took the Georgetown Ferry and found the new black soldiers on pay day. Impressed by their stalwart and disciplined bearing, he wrote later when he saw them parading through the city under arms, that the "Secesh" onlookers were not as insulting as in the past. Their soldierly qualities were confirmed shortly. In the fierce fighting at Port Hudson and Vicksburg, black regiments had done well, holding their positions staunchly, giving and taking heavy losses. There was pride on black faces on Washington streets.

Like everyone else on the delirious day Richmond fell and Washington went mad with joy, blacks danced and paraded through the city streets and on the Arlington House lawns. They too stood in grief and disbelief outside the Petersen House where the President lay dying. On April 19, 1865 a black regiment by happenstance

employment for the able-bodied at the forts, depots, corrals and hospitals. When Duff Green's Row was needed as a prison, its black tenants were moved into a former cavalry barracks, Camp Barker, a full city block bounded by Twelfth and Thirteenth Streets and Q and R Streets NW.

Camp Barker was soon overloaded. To relieve the congestion another black community was established across the Anacostia River in the Hillsdale area. In mid-1863 yet another camp was built across the Potomac

From the roof of Willard's Hotel one could see how the Washington Monument, the nearby city, the Potomac River and the Virginia shore looked in the summer of 1861. Distant tentcamps line the Virginia side.
Martin Luther King Library

led the whole Lincoln funeral procession of 30,000 soldiers to the Capitol. Pennsylvania Avenue was that day a sea of black as well as white faces. These black Americans had lived in powerful and fearful times. They had personally witnessed 200 years of bondage crash down in the fires of civil war. Yet theirs was the fate of living on with high hopes of freedom blasted in the realities of discrimination and poverty which their reunited country seemed unable to end.

A Hundred Circling Camps

The first days of hostilities in April of 1861 found Washington a deserted camp. Only a thousand or so Regulars were available for defense; the city's militia was too full of Southerners to be trustworthy.

By April 25, 1861, when the New York Seventh Regiment arrived like saviors, the problem—to plague Washington for the next four war years—was too many soldiers! Arriving on each other's heels that first spring in response to the President's call for troops, regiment after regiment marched jauntily up Pennsylvania Avenue with their proud flags and thundering drums, and then hunted for a place to live.

The city's relief at being so gallantly rescued from a Confederate occupation was soon tinged with alarm. By fall the city was inundated with soldiers and, most citizens realized glumly, would stay that way. During the early months of 1862 over 200,000 men camped in and near the city, more than three times the city's population just twelve months earlier.

First, the troops took shelter under any suitable roof

they could find and lived in the city itself. Later, for reasons of health, discipline, training and the need to separate so many high-spirited boys from the long-suffering civilian population, the regiments shifted to tent camps along the low hills north of Boundary Street (now Florida Avenue).

When the Virginia side of the Potomac was secured for the Union, most regiments shifted south to confront the Confederate Army building up near Manassas. At least two regiments refused to make this move, and were surrounded by Regular Army troops carrying loaded weapons with orders to shoot if necessary. Cowed by such stern measures the unruly regiments submitted. Their colors were taken away in disgrace; their leaders, in manacles, were removed to the Navy Yard, tried and sent off to prison in the Dry Tortugas, remote islands off the southern tip of Florida.

By the fall of 1861 the Virginia hills and Potomac lowlands were white with tents in camps from Arlington Heights to the wooded hills south of Alexandria. The camps couldn't spread very far west because Confederate pickets ambushed and sniped at the unwary near Baileys Crossroads, Falls Church, Vienna and Lewinsville.

Letters and regimental histories tell us what camp life was like. Lt. David R. P. Hibbs of the One Hundred and Fourth Pennsylvania Volunteers wrote his parents that it was "dull monotony." Bugle calls ordered the soldier's life; over twenty a day badgered him every time he tried to sit down. Reveille snatched him from a sound sleep at 5:00 A.M. in the summer. "Peas on a Trencher," a call inherited from the British Army, summoned him abruptly to breakfast. Other calls sounded shortly for guard mount and sick call; then came the dreaded call to drill and drudgery the rest of the morning. A welcome respite arrived when the bugles trilled "Roast Beef" at noon; the men trooped in to the big meal of the day.

After an hour or so, the ever present bugle assembled the men again. Afternoons provided more variety. Large details worked on the forts springing up near the camps; woodchopping details brought in the firewood that kept them warm; others fetched supplies or helped with construction in the city.

The afternoons were occasionally given over to large reviews which the generals and Washington society attended. A huge one took place in the late fall of 1861 near Baileys Crossroads on the Virginia side. President Lincoln and General McClellan reviewed close to 80,000 men. The General was so impressed during the march-by with "the lofty pomposity of Drum Major William Whaley, Sixth Wisconsin, that he took off his cap as Whaley strutted past. Whaley became so overcome that in the middle of a top-loftical

Mess line of Union soldiers. The scene could be near Washington or along the Rappahannock. The third man in line is Walt Whitman. Drawing by war artist Edwin Forbes.

Library of Congress

gyration of his baton, he dropped it!—plunging him into the deepest gulf of despair."

Supper call announced the best part of the day, first food, then relaxation—visiting comrades or writing letters home. All too soon "tattoo" would sound, sending the men to their tents. Then (later in the war) General Dan Butterfield's lovely call "taps" sounded its solemn, haunting notes and the tired young men went to sleep. Accompanying the bugle calls sometimes was a corps of drummers, mostly teen-aged boys, whose noise and clamor shook the countryside.

Thrown together in large numbers, the new soldiers soon developed their own language which baffled civilians. Before the end of 1861, march became hutch, a tent was a canvas, a sword was a toadsticker, beef was salt-horse, coffee became boiled-rye, vegetables were cow-feed, and butter was strong grease.

Running like a dark thread through many letters home were accounts of sickness and epidemics rife in the camps around Washington. When the damp, penetrating cold of the first winter of the war settled over the hundred or more tent and hut camps, nearly everyone came down with colds. Thousands lived close together in the open without benefit of field sanitation. The ranks soon thinned. Dysentery, debilitating fevers, measles to which the farm boys were most vulnerable, typhoid, small pox and cholera struck down many hundreds in the crowded, filthy camps. A strong constitution was essential to staying well. Long before they had a chance to face the bullets of the enemy, many men were invalided home.

Mail and newspapers from home were big events of the soldier's day. Homesick men wrote floods of mail to their families. After a time the wartime mails became astonishingly reliable and fast. It took only one day, for instance, for a letter to come from Bristol, Pennsylvania, to a camp near Washington. The men swore by it—"The mail will follow you anywhere." Families looked for reasons to visit a soldier in the nation's capital. Judging from the volume of letters, many a soldier's absence left an aching void at home.

When soldiers went on pass into Washington, the more serious minded among them were sure to visit the Capitol, wandering about its ornate halls and perhaps

feeling, like Walt Whitman, that so much embellishment was somehow a little un-American. Later they could saunter up Pennsylvania Avenue, buy a small pie or cake near Seventh Street, and then continue on for a glimpse of the White House. Others, free of the restraints of home and looking for excitement, would head directly for the "fleshpots" of Hooker's Division, the Island, Swampoodle, the Northern Liberties or some other notorious haunt. The denizens of Washington's underworld, thieves, illegal liquor vendors, touts, prostitutes and the like, would envelop them like flies. Most of the innocents were soon fleeced of their $13-a-month pay and returned to camp sadder and wiser men. Some, however, plunged in deeper to emerge dirty, battered and broke, at the Central Guard House, in trouble with their Colonel, suffering a hangover and bound for punishment duty.

As the winter neared its end orders arrived; tents were struck, and long, dusty blue columns followed by baggage wagons wound through the streets to the Sixth Street wharves or the docks in Alexandria. Training, and boyhood too, was now over. For many, mortal or

crippling wounds lay ahead. All would soon encounter the searing, shocking experience of battle.

Looking Back in 1865

The war years brought native Washingtonians, and those who came to the city during the four tumultuous war years, the extremes of emotion. For Unionists, first came the high hopes of easy victory. Then followed months of grim endurance—two long years of repeated, massive defeats that struck at Union hearts like hammer blows. Next, the Union fought a year and a half of pitched battles, won at a cost of northern boys killed, wounded and missing that brought her citizens to the brink of despair. The plight of residents who favored the South must have been worse. They had come to the brink of victory again and again, only to have the North struggle back to its feet and press on. They had heard the distant cannon, yet never seen the boys in gray on the streets of Washington, except as prisoners. They had lived in dread that the next message smuggled through the lines would announce the loss of loved ones or friends. And they had seen the South grow ever more strained, exhausted, and, finally, defeated.

On April 3, 1865 fourteen-year-old War Department telegraph operator, Willie Kettles, listened in near shock as his key stuttered out the dateline "Richmond!" The capital of the Confederacy had fallen—the end was at hand! Cannon in Washington's sixty-eight forts thundered out 800 salutes.

The war-weary thousands surged into Washington's streets in the wildest spontaneous celebration the city had ever known. Strangers embraced; flags waved everywhere; crowds paraded and gathered around impromptu band concerts, speeches, illuminations, fireworks, far into the night. Good news continued to pound the capital day after day: Lee Surrenders! President Davis Flees! Johnson Surrenders! Fort Sumter in Union Hands!

The celebration continued day after day. Then, felled by a devastating blow, the nation and the city was suddenly, incredibly, cast into mourning. The President, "Father Abraham," had died at the hands of an assassin.

The end of the war found the city dirtier and more bedraggled than ever before, but it had become in fact what it was always supposed to be—the capital, acknowledged by all, of the United States. Many Ameri-

Grand Review on the plain east of the Capitol, Fall of '61.
National Archives

cans fighting in Virginia or manning the defenses of Washington had had a personal role in defending the city. Others in distant regiments, forts or ships felt they had done their part in preserving the Union and its capital. For millions of people far from the war zone the city's impact was just as great—what happened in or near Washington was headline news day after day, discussed by everyone from Maine to California.

Washington had been at the vortex of the struggle to save the Union and become the visible sign of its success. The national agony that followed the President's murder not only sanctified Mr. Lincoln, but his capital city as well. From all these great events, sorrows, sacrifices, strivings and powerful emotions emerged a national consensus. Washington had become the symbol of the nation.

Temporary quarters of the 69th New York (a famous Irish Regiment) at Georgetown College in Spring, 1861. At this time the arriving Union troops lived in the city, anywhere they could.

National Archives

PART II

The Downtown City Tour

Tour A.

MAP 5.

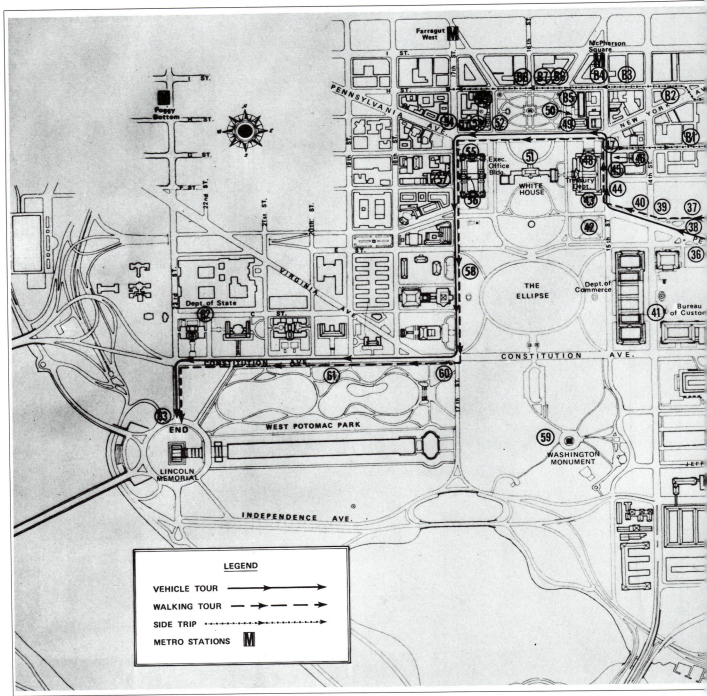

Points of Civil War Interest in Downtown Washington. Tour Routes A and B.

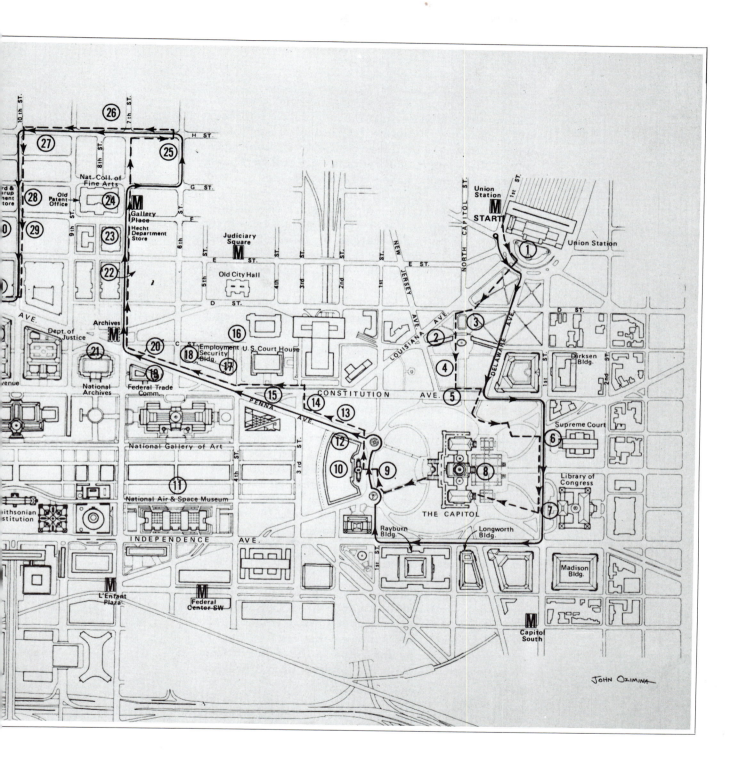

How to Use this Guide

Among the massive sandstone and marble buildings of modern Washington is hidden a surprising amount of the old Civil War city of Mr. Lincoln's day. Many of the important buildings are still here, and where many more have vanished, the sites are still identifiable.

With this Guide, these old places are easy to find. Turn to the map on the preceding page. The vehicle and walking tours are marked by solid and dotted arrows respectively. Along the route are circled numbers, each marking the place where some interesting events occurred.

To use the system, choose a circled number, then turn to the same number found at the top of the pages of the text. Or turn to the same number in the Table of Contents which will give you a page reference.

If you wish to follow the entire central city tour, about an hour's time by vehicle, start at the Union Station (No. 1) and follow the arrows to the Lincoln Memorial (No. 63), a distance of about five miles. For driving, the ideal touring time is on the weekend when traffic is light. During weekdays, avoid the rush hours by going between 10:00 a.m. and 4:00 p.m.

To assist walkers, the central city tour is broken into parts, each with a special appeal. At the beginning of each part is a portion of the map which identifies it and its points of interest. Metro Stops have been marked for your convenience.

A side trip has been added to the G and H Street area where many prominent people lived and several important events occurred.

Some places of significance during the Civil War are widely scattered throughout the city and not conveniently included on the downtown tour. I have suggested a few of general interest that can be visited by car. Their locations are found in the Table of Contents in Part IV—"Sites of Interest in and near the City."

Since the tour is arranged geographically, the stories which enliven and explain each site cannot be in chronological order. This could confuse some readers, and therefore a Chronology of Civil War events involving Washington is included in the Appendix.

Remember, this tour has been planned for you to see not only what the old Civil War city was like, but at the same time to take in the splendors of a great, modern capital and world center as well.

ENJOY YOURSELVES!

The Union Station is one of the splendid buildings of Washington. Finished in 1908, it consolidated all the rail lines serving Washington into one terminal.

Susan C. Lee

UNION STATION AND NATIONAL CAPITOL AREA

Vehicle Tour—Start in front of the Union Station and drive south on Delaware Avenue. Follow the solid black arrows. (Map)

Walking Tour—Start in front of the Union Station and follow the dotted black arrows. (Map)

Services—The quickest, most convenient way to reach the Union Station is to use METRO, getting off at the UNION STATION STOP. Cabs, city buses and the Park Service's Tourmobile can also be used. To leave the area use CAPITOL SOUTH, FEDERAL CENTER SW or JUDICIARY SQUARE METRO STOPS, whichever is more convenient.

Parking other than short-term is hard to find near Union Station. The same is true for lunch accommodations, although the Station does have a fastfood restaurant.

The National Park Service maintains a National Visitor's Center just inside the Station's main doors. Here a wealth of information and free brochures are available on accommodations in the city and historic places to visit. Nearby in the Station is the Park Service's National Book Store with an excellent selection of books and pamphlets on subjects of interest to tourists.

When you reach the vicinity of the U. S. Capitol, the shortage of parking is apparent. However, there are two-hour parking places available on the streets to the east of the Library of Congress buildings, if you are willing to search for them.

Good lunches at reasonable prices in pleasant surroundings can be had at the South (Visitor's) Cafeteria in the Dirksen Senate Office Building north of the Capitol, the Rayburn and Longworth House Office Buildings south of the Capitol, and the Madison Building of the Library of Congress east of the Capitol. All are closed on Sunday.

MAP 6.

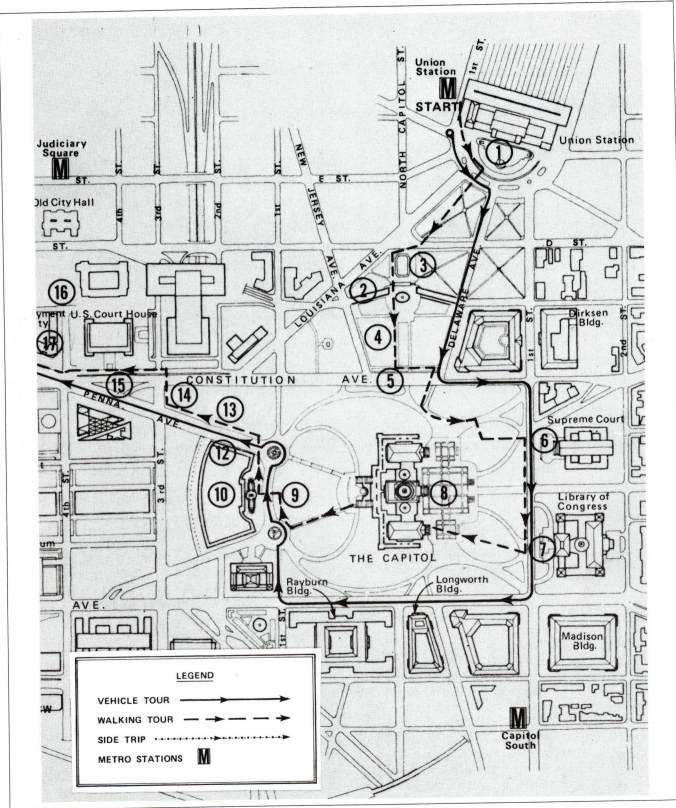

Union Station and National Capitol Area. Central City Tour begins (Tour A).

1.

Union Station (Swampoodle)

Notice the marble facade of Union Station, built at the turn of the century in the Beaux Arts classical style, then try to imagine what was there in Civil War days—the southern fringes of the straggling, disreputable shantytown of Swampoodle. Notorious for an unhealthy, swampy location on the banks of Tiber Creek, its dirtiness, crime and dubious loyalty to the Union, Swampoodle was the ideal place to turn a dishonest dollar.

Patrick Quirk, like most of his neighbors, was Irish and not long from the "ould sod." But unlike them, on June 2, 1862, he had just voted for Richard Wallach, the Republican candidate for Mayor. Hearing this, his irate neighbor, Mary Shaunnessy, broke through his front door, blistered him for a damned Republican, and then stripped to the buff as her ultimate gesture of contempt. Paralyzed with shock, he watched her fall to her knees and "pray that his children be born blind, and that purgatory would hold him fast." (Leech, *Reveille in Washington*) The police carted her off to the "Blue Jug" (city jail); they had also captured her brother who was after other Republicans with a double-barreled shotgun.

Violence, dirt and lots of activity were part of the typical day in Swampoodle. With evening's approach, certain young ladies sauntered by; police and provost marshal patrols took up their beats; a pronounced exodus of men and women headed for the nearby Army camps and railroad yards with larceny in their hearts. Every evening they sold illicit whiskey, gambled and cheated the soldiers any way they could. In one shack or another around town the local criminal aristocracy worked hard at the business of fencing stolen government horses, guns and especially medicines like quinine. Some wartime fortunes began in these surroundings.

Young soldiers in blue gathered in the muddy streets and alleys, like lambs for the slaughter, oblivious to warnings that Swampoodle was no safe place at night.

2.

The Old Baltimore & Ohio Railroad Station

Going south on Delaware Avenue, look to your right after crossing D Street. On the opposite side of the park (Union Station Plaza), about where Louisiana and New Jersey Avenues intersect, lies the site of the old Baltimore and Ohio Railroad Station.

Long gone, the depot was an exciting place during the war—the terminal of the city's lifeline by land to the north. Here arrived and departed daily most of the soldiers and supplies that fueled the Union War effort in Virginia.

On April 25, 1861 the citizens of Washington felt isolated; the telegraph line had been cut, and rail travel interrupted. People were frightened. Businesses ground to a halt, food was scarce, and the roads north swarmed with buggies and wagons filled with people searching for a haven. Among the whispered rumors was one that Virginians would soon capture the city.

Worried crowds gathered at the station hoping for news from the north. At about 5:00 p.m. a train pulled in with a regiment on board—the Sixth Massachusetts. Its soldiers confirmed the fearful rumors: tumultuous prosouthern crowds *had* attacked the regiment in Baltimore. Washingtonians gaped at the sight of the four dead and thirty-one wounded men carried off the cars. A few volunteers hurried forward to give what medical care they could. Clara Barton, later to found the American Red Cross, was among them.

The soldiers formed up and marched smartly behind their band to the nearby Capitol where they bivouacked in the ornate luxury of the Senate Chamber itself. The new President, dispirited by the city's isolation and other pressing worries, spoke to some of them a few days later. Said Lincoln: "I don't believe there is any North . . . Rhode Island is not known in our geography any longer. *You* are the only northern realities."

This view of Swampoodle seems more respectable than the village of Civil War days. Tiber Creek, an open sewer, is shown with the bridges at G and H Streets. Both were demolished when Tiber Creek was filled over in 1876. The location is just north of the present Union Station.   *Martin Luther King Library*

The old Baltimore and Ohio Railroad Station, built in 1851, stood on the northwest corner of North Capitol and C Streets. Both streets at this intersection and the Station too were demolished to become part of the Union Station Plaza. Shown here is the 71st New York Regiment, marching in style behind its band, on its way to temporary billets at the U.S. Navy Yard at Eighth and M Streets SE.

National Archives

3.
The Soldier's Rest

Glance to the right as you move south on Delaware Avenue from D to C Streets. The former site of the Soldier's Rest covered the near side of this park (Union Station Plaza) and stretched across Delaware Avenue to the east. This transient soldier camp was the forerunner of many other such camps during the Civil and later wars.

By the early summer of 1861, though the war was barely three months old, Washington had become a bedlam of arriving troops. Most came by train. The civilian community was concerned. Soldiers arrived tired and hungry; some lay sick and uncared for in the station. Lost in a strange city, neither men nor officers knew how to obtain food and shelter for themselves.

On July 2, 1861 a harassed Union Army took over the Mount Vernon Cane Factory, the long, low building once situated a few yards east of the old Baltimore & Ohio Station. Here a corps of cooks and waiters set about feeding the incoming and departing soldiers around the clock. When word of an arriving troop train came by telegraph, a platoon of cooks and helpers went into action—cutting and cooking meat and vegetables, preparing tables, and, above all, readying the indispensable coffee. When the troops arrived, they sat down to a hot meal. If they were to move on into Virginia, they received a day's ration after the meal.

By 1862 a larger feeding hall became necessary in order to serve 800 men at a time. Around the new hall sprang up barracks, storage and dispensary facilities. At the height of the war The Rest once fed sixteen regiments (8,000 to 12,000 men) in one 24-hour period. Prisoners of war also ate here before they started their long trek under guard to prison camps. Soldiers' diaries sometimes mentioned this stopover; one or two complained that the food was greasy.

When the war ended the troops quickly vanished

from Washington. Baltimore & Ohio passenger traffic to and from the city fell off by half, and The Rest closed its doors in October 1865.

4.
The Home Lodge of the Sanitary Commission

In this same park, near the junction of Delaware and Constitution Avenues, is the site of the now-vanished Home Lodge of the Sanitary Commission, run by that very special, caring man, Mr. Frederick Knapp.

On August 9, 1861, Mr. Knapp, an Associate Secretary of the newly founded Sanitary Commission, made a search through the railroad cars on one of the sidings near the Baltimore & Ohio Station. While thus following up a rumor of trouble, he came upon thirty-six sick soldiers from an Indiana regiment who had not eaten for twenty-four hours. From a nearby hotel he bought two pails of tea and a half-bushel of bread and butter for the famished men. He stayed with them himself until ambulances arrived. Now alerted, Knapp prowled through the station and cars daily, and often found other neglected men.

He persuaded the Army to assign him a small corner of the newly opened Soldier's Rest (next to the station), and there started a small hospital. Within a few days the Army took back the space for its own needs. Knapp immediately rented a large house close by at 374 North Capitol Street. That same evening twenty-one invalid soldiers slept there. Up to ninety patients were housed here on some nights.

The heavy toll of great battles was felt widely by mid-1862. Mr. Knapp noticed enfeebled discharged soldiers wandering about the city. Sometimes disoriented in their distress, they desperately needed help in such simple matters as collecting their pay, buying their train tickets and finding the right train home. Moreover, these victims of the war fell prey to a multitude of conmen gathered outside the Army Pay Office to fleece them as they came out. Knapp rescued them from the streets and gathered them at the Home Lodge. Providing protection, food and rest, he got them their pay, bought their tickets and put them on the right trains. In this way hundreds of shocked often helpless men were returned safely to their homes and families.

The Sanitary Commission had been started in 1861 by private citizens who banded together to help the overwhelmed government provide badly needed care to the Union soldier. Arousing and mobilizing the entire North, the Commission raised millions of dollars at fairs and through contributions. The money bought special medical supplies, foods, clothing and services designed to improve the soldier's hard life. Aid reached the men through "lodges" and "shebangs" in cities, hospitals, camps and near the front—wherever large numbers of soldiers were brought together.

The Home Lodge of the Sanitary Commission, as it looked during the war, was located on North Capitol Street near its junction with B Street (now Constitution Avenue). The buildings and street too are now gone, and the space is a part of Union Station Plaza.
Library of Congress

5.
Escape Route of President Lincoln's Assassin

Turn left off Delaware Avenue and east on Constitution Avenue for one block to First Street NE.

At about 10:30 on the damp moonless night of April 14, 1865, John Wilkes Booth, a popular, handsome actor and scion of a famous acting family, galloped east down this stretch of Constitution Avenue (then B Street) as he fled from Ford's Theater.

Wartime photo of the Navy Yard Bridge at Eleventh and O Streets SE. The check point where Sergeant Cobb stopped Booth would have been at the near end of the bridge.

National Archives

Fifteen minutes earlier he had shot President Lincoln in the back of the head. Then, after stabbing Major Rathbone, a theater guest of the Lincolns, he jumped from the theater box onto the stage below. The spur of his boot caught in the folds of a flag, breaking his leg. He limped across the stage brandishing his knife at the stunned actors on stage and in the wings. After leaving the theater by the rear entrance, he mounted with difficulty a fast horse, and then made his way through a back alley to F Street.

The remainder of his escape route is conjecture, though many authorities think he galloped east on F Street and then southeast on New Jersey Avenue to B Street (now Constitution Avenue). Turning right onto First Street NE, he headed for Pennsylvania Avenue and then followed it to the Navy Yard Bridge which led into Southern Maryland.

Stopped at the bridge by Union Sergeant Silas T. Cobb, the sentry on duty, he was allowed to pass through because of relaxed attitudes since the war's end. Booth's escape, however, only prolonged his ordeal. As the object of a tremendous search, he was run to ground ten days later in a tobacco barn near Port Royal, Virginia. In the confusion of burning the barn to bring him out, Booth was shot and killed.

History obscures what happened to Sergeant Cobb when War Secretary Stanton learned he had let the assassin escape. One suspects he was lucky if he only "lost his stripes."

6.
The Old Capitol Prison

The site of the Old Capitol Prison on the southeast corner of First Street NE and Maryland Avenue is the present location of the U.S. Supreme Court building.

The Old Capitol, built in 1814, housed Congress after the British burned the original Capitol. When Congress returned to the rebuilt Capitol, this temporary Capitol became a boardinghouse. Among its tenants was the standard-bearer of the Old South, Senator John C. Calhoun, who died here in 1850.

During the war the Old Capitol, together with neighboring buildings—Duff Green's and Carroll Row—became a prison. Stories about the place are endless. It was damp, dirty and crowded with captured southern soldiers, contrabands, spies, criminals, cashiered Union officers, and sometimes as many as 200 political prisoners from Washington and Georgetown. People looked with dread upon the place, because any citizen could find himself there without warning or legal appeal. Mr. Lincoln had suspended the writ of *habeas corpus.*

Among the inmates were Mrs. Greenhow and Belle Boyd, celebrated southern spies. Both were women of charm and intellect, always at the center of continuing intrigue, sympathy and hostility. General McClellan is supposed to have said of the former, "She knows my plans better than Lincoln." True heroines of the South, they enjoyed their roles immensely, and when finally sent to Richmond, probably missed the excitement of center stage at the prison.

On November 10, 1865, Captain Henry Wirz, CSA, Commandant of infamous Andersonville Prison in Georgia, stood on the scaffold in the prison yard. Soldiers were drawn up with the press and public peering over their shoulders. The drummers beat slowly, the trap dropped, the body swung. The North felt that justice was done on behalf of 13,000 Union prisoners of war who had died lingering deaths of hunger, privation and disease at Andersonville.

Within two years after the war the Old Capitol was torn down. No one regretted the disappearance of a place burdened with so many evil memories.

7.
Congressman Lincoln's Boardinghouse

Where the Library of Congress is now on First Street NE once stood Carroll Row, a group of five large row houses facing the Capitol. They were among the earliest homes in Washington.

During the British capture of the city in 1814, Carroll Row was a hospital for wounded British soldiers, left behind when the Red Coats marched back to their ships. The Row became an annex to the Old Capitol Prison during the Civil War.

During the Civil War the Old Capitol Prison stood on the southeast corner of First Street and Maryland Avenue NE. It was the most important prison in the city. Notice the sentries on their beats.

Library of Congress

The third house from the left (photo) was Mrs. Anna G. Sprigg's boardinghouse where Abraham Lincoln lived as a one-term Congressman (1848–1849). He liked Mrs. Sprigg's place where boarded other Congressmen like himself. At the dinner table Lincoln relished storytelling. He always approached a story the same way. Putting down his knife and fork, he would place his elbows on the table and hold his face between both large hands. "That reminds me," he would start. All readied themselves for an uproar. On a free evening, Lincoln would sometimes persuade a friend to go bowling with him.

The new Congressman had a close look at the ugliness of slavery. Occasionally groups of black slaves in chains passed through the streets. Near the Capitol was a jail which was, in Lincoln's words, "a sort of Negro Livery Stable" where blacks were kept while awaiting shipment south "precisely like a drove of horses." At his own boardinghouse a black servant, who had paid all but $60 of the $300 price for his freedom, was seized by two men, carried off to a slave pen, then sent to the auction block in New Orleans. An effort by Mr. Lincoln and his friends to redress this injustice in the House of Representatives failed.

Today on this same corner one of Washington's finest edifices, the Supreme Court building, now stands. *Susan C. Lee*

Carroll Row, seen here in its Civil War setting, was torn down about 1885 for the construction of the Library of Congress. Congressman Lincoln's boardinghouse was the third from the left.

Library of Congress

8.
The Capitol

Turn your back on the Library of Congress and you are looking directly west at the Capitol of the United States through its park.

Few people wandering through the Capitol realize the unlikely uses to which this historic place was put during the Civil War:

A Fort—In April of 1861 when Union authorities feared the city was in imminent danger of capture, field guns frowned from ceremonial entrances, heavy iron plates intended for the new dome were upended in hallways as breastworks; soldiers manned defense positions, and through the night sentries trod their beats along the silent halls.

A Barracks—The first large Federal forces to arrive in the city were brought to the Capitol in late April of 1861. Thomas Winthrop of the Seventh New York, who was to die within a year at the Battle of Big Bethel, left an account of the Regiment's move into the House chamber. The staff took the committee rooms; the Colonel bedded down in the ornate Speaker's parlor.

A Bakery—More soldiers poured into Washington every day during the spring and summer of 1861. They had to be fed. One hundred and fifty bakers worked around the clock in the cellars under the Capitol's west wing producing 60,000 loaves a day. These were carted off by lines of wagons waiting outside, bound for the camps springing up about Washington.

A Hospital—The Second Battle of Bull Run and the Battle of Antietam in August and September of 1862 brought the city a multitude of wounded men, far more

than the hospitals in Washington, Georgetown and Alexandria could accommodate. Two thousand cots were hurriedly set up in the Senate and House chambers, along the corridors and in the rotunda. They were hardly in place before a thousand sufferers from Bull Run were brought to the House chamber. Fortunately, Congress was not in session.

In their season the Congressmen took over, enduring a special harassment. Marble blocks scattered about amidst scaffolding impeded movement, but the new, stately dome, to be topped by the gleaming figure of "Armed Freedom," slowly climbed toward completion. When criticized for spending money on the Capitol during the war, President Lincoln responded, "It is a sign we intend the Union to go on."

The press on a Washington story—observing the execution of Captain Wirz (Commandant of Andersonville Prison), at the Old Capitol Prison, November 10, 1865. *Martin Luther King Library*

This fine print from the *Illustrated London News* (May, '61) shows the unfinished Capitol and the western part of the downtown city. →

National Archives

A splendid moment, the day of Lincoln's Second Inaugural (March 4, 1865), was dark and dripping with rain. A newspaperman, Noah Brooks, reported that as the President held up his hand to take the oath of office "the sun burst through the clouds, splashing the Capitol steps with brilliant light." Lincoln thought it a good omen. "Did you see that sunburst?", he remarked later. "It made my heart jump!"

Standing behind the President on the Inaugural platform was John Wilkes Booth, the actor, seeking an opportunity to stab Mr. Lincoln and escape. Other conspirators were among the crowd below. In about five weeks Booth would succeed in killing the President at Ford's Theater.

9.

The Washington and Alexandria Railroad

In the center of First Street NW, running between the Grant Memorial and the Capitol, were once the tracks of the Washington and Alexandria Railroad.

The Capitol as barracks. The Eighth Massachusetts Regiment has settled down in the Rotunda. Other regiments lived in the House and Senate chambers (Spring, 1861).

Martin Luther King Library

The Washington and Alexandria Railroad. The scene is on First Street NW as people leave the Capitol after the daily ajournment.

Library of Congress

From the Baltimore & Ohio Station the rails ran south on First Street, southwest on Maryland Avenue to the Long Bridge across the Potomac, and terminated at the Alexandria Station.

Bear in mind that the Civil War was the first war in history in which railroads were in general use by both sides. This short, five-mile track became vital to the Union. It was the only connection in the eastern United States between the Northern and Southern rail systems. Moreover, it was the all-important rail entry into Virginia, the primary theater of war (Map 7).

Trains steaming from Washington or Alexandria could run (1) to the southwest on the Orange and Alexandria Railroad to the great battlegrounds of the Rappahannock and Rapidan areas, (2) to the west on the Manassas Gap Railroad into the beautiful but devastated Valley of Virginia, and (3) to the northwest on the Alexandria and Loudoun Railroad to Leesburg with its important military crossing sites over the upper Potomac.

These railroads performed crucial service to the Union. But tracks were constantly torn up and rebuilt as the armies and partisans moved about them. In the early war years the North lost engines and rolling stock when rail junctions like Manassas and Warrenton fell suddenly to Confederate forces. Wartime photographs of engines and cars wrecked and burned testify to the vulnerability of railroads in fought-over country.

The Union learned by experience; if danger threatened, the trains were hurried to safety. A sign that Lee's Army was rampaging not far from Washington was the large number of engines and cars crowded into the haven of the Maryland Avenue railroad yards.

MAP 7.

Vital Rail Net and the Great Battle Grounds in Virginia.

The Baltimore and Ohio Railroad connects Washington to the North. To the south the Washington and Alexandria Railroad, only five miles long, connects Washington with the Orange and Alexandria Railroad, the only rail link between the northern and southern rail systems in the eastern U.S. The latter runs southwest through Virginia to link up with the whole rail net of the South.

The shaded part shows the area of great battles. While some of the most important battles were fought elsewhere, this terrain marks the most foughtover, bloodsoaked grounds of the whole war. Over 300,000 men were killed, wounded or missing here.

10.
The Grant Memorial

First Street NW at the western foot of Capitol Hill facing the Mall.

Hunching forward in the saddle, General Grant looks silently down the Mall in Henry Shrady's fine sculpture.

Library of Congress

On May 14, 1864 near Spotsylvania Courthouse, a young artilleryman, Private Reed, from Bigelow's Ninth Massachusetts Battery, stood to his gun watching General Grant on horseback nearby survey the spectacle of war. The battlefield stretched out before Grant was alive with moving columns of men, horses, wagons and artillery—all shifting their positions to resume the attack. Private Reed quickly sketched the General.

It is much the same pose that sculptor Henry Shrady chose for the Grant Memorial. The General is astride his favorite horse, Cincinnati, slouching, shoulders hunched forward, hand on hip, staring grimly down the Mall. The pose captures the silent determination and patience that marked the man. His Army took such terrible losses it staggered the Union; yet he never turned back, persisting till final victory.

The splendid action groups that flank the Grant statue are certainly the most vivid, authentic sculptures

Shrady's exciting sculpture of Union Cavalry in a hot action and at the charge.

Library of Congress

Dr. Lowe's gas generating wagons are grouped near his deflated balloon "Enterprise" on the Mall. On June 18, 1861 Dr. Lowe made the first aerial flight over Washington from this location, a spectacular event in the city's history.   *Library of Congress*

of galloping artillery and cavalry troopers to be found in this country. By showing what moments of intense combat and total exertion must have looked like, Shrady left something priceless to generations who never knew the Civil War firsthand. He died of exhaustion just before his sculpture was dedicated.

11.
The Mall and Washington's First Aerial Flight

As you stand at the Grant Memorial looking west, before you stretches the Mall, one of the majestic sights of this country.

During the Civil War it was a large tract of waste ground, obstructed here and there by eyesores like the City Canal and the gas works. The latter had simply moved in unchallenged. Few people, including Congressmen, knew it as the National Mall, a centerpiece in Major L'Enfant's original plan for the city. Not an entirely safe place, it was frequented by criminals, outcasts and vagrants. The Army and others grazed cattle and other domestic animals there.

Coincidentally, about where the white marble National Air and Space Museum stands, the nearest building on the south (left) side of the Mall, there occurred the first aerial flight in Washington and man's first air-to-ground message. Dr. Thaddeus Sobieski Constantine Lowe, showman and balloonist extraordinaire at 29, prepared to erect his giant balloon *Enterprise* (20,-000 cubic feet) on June 18, 1861.

Soaring to 500 feet, Dr. Lowe looked down on the Capitol and the panorama beneath him. Using a telegraph line to the ground, he sent a message to President Lincoln at the White House:

Dear Sir: This point of observation commands an area nearly fifty miles in diameter. The city, with its girdle of encampments, presents a superb scene. I have pleasure in sending you this first dispatch ever telegraphed from an aerial station . . .

The balloon was then pulled by its hawser through the streets to the White House grounds for President Lincoln to view it. He did so from an upstairs window.

51

MAP 8.

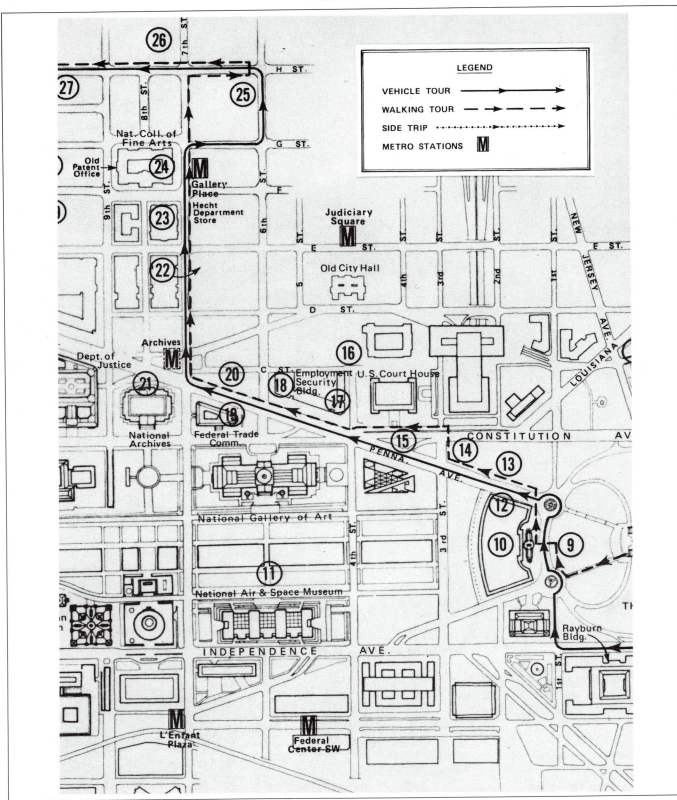

Lower Pennsylvania Avenue, Seventh and H Streets.

President-elect Lincoln and President Buchanan ride down Pennsylvania Avenue enroute to Mr. Lincoln's Inaugural ceremony, March 4, 1861. The fate of the Union looked black.

National Archives

LOWER PENNSYLVANIA AVENUE—SEVENTH STREET AREA

Vehicle Tour —Continue northwest up Pennsylvania Avenue to Seventh Street, turn right (north) up Seventh Street to G Street, detour one block to the right, then north one block to H Street. Turn left to see Mrs. Surratt's boardinghouse (left side) and go three blocks to Tenth Street. Prepare to turn left (south) on Tenth Street for next tour segment.

Walking Tour —Walk up Pennsylvania Avenue, preferably on the right side. Turn right at Seventh Street and walk north to H Street. Walk right half a block on H Street to see Mrs. Surratt's boardhouse, then turn around and head west for three blocks to Tenth Street.

Services—If picking up the tour on lower Pennsylvania Avenue, the JUDICIARY SQUARE METRO STOP is closest. If arriving or departing the tour near the Patent Office, use GALLERY PLACE METRO STOP.

Parking lots are few in the lower Pennsylvania Avenue area until you reach about Sixth Street. From this point on up the Avenue, numerous lots are located in the blocks north of the Avenue. It is rare to find a parking place along Pennsylvania and Constitution Avenues or in the streets along the Mall. One good parking lot is located under the National Air and Space Museum, but this is some distance from the Tour.

On the lower Avenue the best and most reasonable food can be found in the two cafeterias in the National Gallery of Art on the south side of Pennsylvania Avenue between Third and Seventh Streets. Both are open for lunch weekdays and weekends. For those in the Seventh Street area, Hecht Company store offers good lunches at F and Seventh Streets. In the Patent Office there is a small cafeteria on the main floor in the east wing. In pleasant weather diners like to eat outside in the courtyard of the Patent Office.

Good bookstores on art and architectural subjects are convenient to lunch facilities at the National Gallery of Art and the Patent Office.

Pennsylvania Avenue looked like this four years later, May 23–24, 1865. General Meade's and General Sherman's armies passed through the city in a triumphant victory parade.
Junior League of Washington

12.
Pennsylvania Avenue

Turn northwest from First Street. Ahead lies broad Pennsylvania Avenue stretching toward the White House.

It was the city's main thoroughfare, its business center and the ceremonial avenue of the nation. Far from elegant, it was generally dusty or muddy, paved badly with cobblestones and gas-lit by night. Lined with low frame and brick buildings, it hummed with activity.

The structures on the Avenue's north side were taller and in better repair in the 1860's than those across the street. Its stores were attractive and filled with shoppers; the sidewalks held a moving, bustling throng. The Avenue's south side was more deserted and its buildings less pretentious, some leaning and decrepit. Here one found among boardinghouses, homes, cracker and pie stores and shops, scores of saloons, gambling houses and brothels, a concentration of dubious enterprises of all kinds.

On a fine afternoon the Avenue was a sight to remember. Mixing with the socially elite promenading the north side were political leaders, diplomats, clerks, officers, soldiers, businessmen, etc. Among them were people of every nation, mostly Irish, Germans and Italians, who had made their way to "the land of opportunity." There were also Contrabands (former slaves), Creoles, Latin Americans, Indians and even an occasional Chinese. Crowding among them, bellowing and gesturing, were the herds of hucksters, hawking candy, oysters and fish, roasted chestnuts, soap, pies, cakes. Above the crowd noises sounded the music of organ grinders and street singers in phrases from popular songs like "Dixie," "Ben Bolt," "Captain Jinks," "Shoo-fly." Groups around the shoeshine boys made small eddies among the strollers; conmen and touts talked fast and grabbed arms, while pickpockets slipped skillfully through the crowd. Watching it all at street corners were hard-faced dragoons, mounted with sabres in hand, ready to gallop after "speeders" on horseback.

What one saw at times on the Avenue seemed to portend the coming demise of the Union itself—or a reprieve sent by God.

On March 4, 1861 the frightened city was filled with rumors and plots. As people lined the Avenue to see the President-elect, regulars with loaded rifles watched from the tops of buildings and street corners to protect an already care-worn Mr. Lincoln. Surrounded by horsemen, his carriage bumped its way down the cobblestoned Avenue to his first Inaugural. Outside the city the Union was disintegrating.

Drizzle fell from dawn to dusk on July 22, 1861. The Avenue was packed with thousands of frightened, exhausted and hungry boys in dirty uniforms. Most had lost their units and thrown away their rifles as they fled through the night from the lost battlefield of Bull Run, across the Long Bridge to safety in the city. Some people set up tables on the sidewalks to feed them. With hopes of an easy victory blasted, Union supporters in the city despaired.

There was good news too. On July 4, 1863 throngs gathered on the Avenue to cheer when word reached them that General Lee's Army had been decisively checked at the little Pennsylvania town of Gettysburg. An elated crowd trooped up the Avenue to the White House lawn to celebrate. Perhaps the tide was starting to turn at last.

On July 11, 1864 citizens watched in consternation as wagon loads of refugees drove into the Avenue at Seventh Street; they listened to the thudding of General Early's cannon to the north; a rumor spread, correct this time, that the rebel army had come through Silver Spring, not six miles from the Capitol itself. Who could save the city this time?

Then, with victory won and jubilation everywhere, the city was suddenly in mourning. Great crowds gathered along the Avenue on April 19, 1865 to watch the funeral procession of President Lincoln move slowly

toward the Capitol. The U.S. Twenty-second Regiment (of black Freedmen), returning from the Petersburg Lines, collided with the procession. They faced about smartly and led the whole 30,000-man parade to the Capitol, ranks straight and solid, their band playing the dirge.

The Avenue always provided special sights that caused crowds to gather and stare. Regiments of cavalry trotted by, led by mounted bands of massed bugles and drums. The young veterans sat their horses easily, sabres and carbines jingling, watching the girls. The noise of thousands of hooves striking the cobbles had a hypnotic effect upon the watchers.

Long, dense columns of infantry moved slowly on the Avenue sometimes taking hours to pass. Each young soldier carried a blanket roll; often a frying pan dangled from his belt, and he held a shiny rifle on his shoulder. He was lean and worn, generally bearded and wearing a jaunty cap. Hooting drovers prodded along immense dust-covered droves of cattle, food for the army. Long, rumbling wagon trains and gleaming battalions of horse artillery were everyday sights; groups of conscripts straggled by under close guard. Provost marshal patrols checked passes; the flow of ambulances with its freight of mangled men barely ceased by day or night; columns of ragged prisoners and deserters dragged by slowly with their guards. It happened all the time.

Lower Pennsylvania Avenue in flood, November, 1861.
Library of Congress

13.
Tiber Creek

Pennsylvania Avenue crossed Tiber Creek (now a covered sewer) at Second Street on an unsafe wooden bridge, with "sometimes handrails and sometimes none." The Creek then flowed sluggishly into the nearby City Canal.

The lowest elevation on the Avenue, the Tiber Creek crossing was the center of occasional severe flooding of the lower city. Starting at First Street rows of small, narrow buildings lined the Avenue on the north side, mostly boardinghouses.

The retirement of aged war hero General Winfield Scott, General-in-Chief of the Army, coincided with one of these unhappy inundations. Early on the dark, foggy morning of November 2, 1861, the General's carriage splashed down the rainy, flooded Pennsylvania Avenue to the Baltimore & Ohio depot. His successor, General McClellan, and an escort of cavalry hunched in long raincloaks, trotted behind to do final honors and goodbys.

The flood's details were reported in *The Evening Star.*

For days heavy rains had swelled the Potomac. The pilings of the Long Bridge backed up excess water east along the City Canal where it met the descending freshet of swollen Tiber Creek. From Second to Sixth Streets, Pennsylvania Avenue was under water. Sewers and basements overflowed, emptying their noxious contents into the muddy, stagnant waters. Lumber dealers near the Canal watched quantities of timber and firewood float away. And as a tragic reminder of the recent defeat at Ball's Bluff near Leesburg, bodies of Union soldiers had washed down the Potomac and been found floating near the Georgetown and Sixth Street wharves.

14.
Walt Whitman's Boardinghouse

Between Second and Third Streets on the north side of the Avenue was in Civil War times a block filled with boardinghouses, small stores, hotels and homes, all a little run down. Today these mostly brick buildings have long vanished; occupying their site are the trees and lawns of Capitol Park.

During the spring of 1864 Walt Whitman (poet, occasional war correspondent, part-time government clerk and full-time friend of the men in the hospitals) lived for $7.00 a month in a third floor bedroom facing the Avenue at about mid-block. This room located him near Armory Square Hospital just across the Mall on the present site of the National Air & Space Museum (Seventh Street and Independence Avenue). Because of its nearness to the Sixth Street wharves and the Maryland Avenue Rail Station, Armory Square received the worst cases of sick and wounded men.

On June 7, 1864 Whitman wrote of the men coming to Armory Square Hospital: "A horrible collection, the worst cases you ever saw; the wounded arrived from the Wilderness so neglected that it is awful, wounds swelled, inflamed, full of worms. Many amputations have to be done over again. A new feature, many are out of their senses—suffered too much."

In a letter of June 14, 1864 to his mother he wrote, "My boardinghouse, 502 Pennsylvania Avenue, is a miserable place—very bad air." There was truth in this. About half a block away at Second Street was filthy Tiber Creek, and across Pennsylvania Avenue two blocks away was the equally stagnant dirty water of the City Canal in this lowest, most pestiferous part of the city.

A post Civil War view of the *St. Charles Hotel,* later known as the *New Capitol.* The slave pens were actually under the sidewalk in front of the hotel shown facing B Street (now Constitution Avenue).   *Martin Luther King Library*

Matthew Brady photograph of Walt Whitman.   *National Archives*

15.
Saint Charles Hotel

On the northwest corner of Third Street and Constitution Avenue, the present locality of the U. S. Courthouse, stood, in Civil War days, one of the fine hotels of the city, the Saint Charles.

Lincoln's Vice-President Hannibal Hamlin lived here. Before the war it was a popular place for well-to-do plantation owners and prosperous slave dealers. The following note to guests was posted in the hotel corridors:

The Proprietor of this hotel has roomy underground cells for confining slaves for safekeeping, and patrons are notified that their slaves will be well cared for. In case of escape, full value of the negro will be paid by the Proprietor.

16.
The Old City Hall

Arriving at the corner of Pennsylvania Avenue and Fourth Street, glance up John Marshall Place to the right (north) and you will see the Grecian portico of the old City Hall, about two blocks away.

On the morning of August 24, 1861, City Hall clerks, indeed the whole city, was buzzing with the incredible news. The Army Provost Marshal on the evening before had arrested no less than Washington's mayor, the Honorable James G. Berret, himself. Accused of treasonable practices, he had allegedly refused to take the oath of allegiance to the United States, a story later proved correct.

The Mayor was hurried off to the Baltimore & Ohio Station early in the morning and found himself on his way north to imprisonment at Fort Lafayette in New York harbor. His confinement lasted three weeks. He was released after taking the prescribed loyalty oath and agreeing to step down as mayor. President Lincoln was troubled by Mayor Berret's misadventure. Later by way of making amends, he first offered him a colonelcy, then the post of Commissioner for the compensated emancipation of the District's slaves. Congress had freed the slaves of District residents on April 16, 1862. The ex-mayor refused both offers.

Runaway slaves being held in Washington's jail on Judiciary Square—known as the "Blue Jug," December, 1861.
National Archives

Mayor Berret had worked in Old City Hall, one of Washington's most graceful buildings. In the Greek Revival style, it was built well before the Civil War. Its architect, George Hadfield, had also designed stately Arlington House, home of the Lees.

The City Hall has housed many tenants over the years. It served occasionally as a slave market before 1850, a Civil War fort briefly in 1861, an army hospital from September to December 1862, and as the home of the U.S. Patent Office. It has been, and is today, a hub of the Federal and District courts system. Its grounds, even in Civil War days, were known as Judiciary Square.

17.
Pennsylvania Avenue Horsecars

Chartered by Congress, the Washington and Georgetown Railway Company began operations in August 1862 down the center of Pennsylvania Avenue between the Capitol and Willard's Hotel.

Starting with only two horse-drawn cars, this new service proved immensely popular. Before long numbers of streetcars were driving the rails between the Navy Yard and Georgetown, about five miles.

It was now easy and cheap to get up and down the Avenue in all kinds of weather. But there were other difficulties. One still had to walk through the dust or mud, always present like the proverbial plagues of Egypt, to enter or leave the cars. Male riders were heard to mutter imprecations against women in crinolines who took up so many seats. The chivalry of those years made a man's standing to give a woman passenger his seat obligatory.

A new kind of racial discrimination appeared. Horse cars soon bore large signs reading "Colored Persons may ride in this car." They were denied entrance to all other cars. Major Augusta, a black surgeon of the 7th Infantry Regiment, wearing the uniform of a U.S. Army officer, was compelled by a conductor to leave a horse car while on his way to testify as a witness at a court martial. After a long walk through rain and slush, he arrived late. The court was given the reasons for his tardiness, and the matter was eventually brought to the attention of the Senate. In the resultant uproar a resolution was passed which threatened revocation of the company's franchise. The signs disappeared.

The Avenue's traffic was another hazard. Not infrequently cars were halted by long wagon trains turning into the Avenue from Seventh Street. Herds of cattle, and sometimes long columns of marching men, surrounded the new streetcars on all sides. The soldiers would stare curiously at these contraptions and their riders as they marched by.

18.
The National Hotel

The National Hotel was located on the northeast corner of Sixth Street and Pennsylvania Avenue. It was torn down in the 1930's.

In the years before the Civil War the spacious National (ten parlors, eight single and fifty double rooms) was the traditional gathering place for southern leaders, just as Willard's, up the Avenue, served the same purpose for their northern counterparts. People remembered that the popular Henry Clay had died while a resident at the National in 1852.

In May and June of 1861 there was a general exodus from the hotel of prominent southerners leaving Congress and the Executive Branch to take up new posts in the Confederate States. Carriages piled high with baggage and bearing southern gentry trotted off daily from the hotel's pillared portico bound for the Sixth Street wharves. The travelers steamed some fifty miles south on the placid Potomac to Aquia Creek, then went by railroad to Richmond and the South.

On December 4, 1863 Washington notables gathered

Print of old City Hall as it looked during the Civil War and as it looks today.

National Archives

here for a dinner to celebrate the long-awaited arrival of Potomac water from Great Falls carried by aqueduct to the city. Mayor Wallach's address fully reflected the general satisfaction: "From this day forth, those who drink good liquor will have good water to go with it, and those of us who drink water only will have good water for that purpose."

In the early months of 1865 sinister events fermented at the National. Because of its southern atmosphere the young actor, John Wilkes Booth, always stayed here when in town. He generally took a room on the second floor in the rear of the hotel. When he wanted a horse he would open the window and whistle in the direction of the livery stable just across the way on C Street. At least some of the plot, first to abduct, and later to murder the President, must have developed here.

19.
Judge McCook's Tragedy

Near the southwest corner of Sixth Street and Pennsylvania Avenue once stood Mrs. Paris' boardinghouse; now the whole block is taken up by the Federal Trade Commission.

On July 28, 1861, Judge Daniel McCook pulled up in front of his residence at Mrs. Paris' boardinghouse. In his wagon lay the body of his 17-year-old son, Charles, a soldier of the Second Ohio Regiment, killed at the First Battle of Bull Run a few days before.

In the absence of news of his son the worried father

The National Hotel during the war years.

Junior League of Washington

The Federal Trade Commission now takes up the whole block between Sixth and Seventh Streets on the Avenue's south side. During the war the block was occupied by boarding houses, shops, homes and small eating places.
Susan C. Lee

had finally driven out to Bull Run. He had searched through the wreckage and horror of the field until he found the body of his son. A sympathetic crowd of neighbors and onlookers gathered as the remains were carried inside.

Judge McCook was a dedicated Union man who had reared seven sons. All served in the Union Army, ranging from Alexander, who became a general, to Charles, a private. The Judge lost his own life in battle two years later.

20.
Brady's National Photographic Art Gallery

In mid-block after passing Sixth Street look for an old brick four-story building on the right (north), Nos. 627 Pennsylvania Avenue.

This drab old building, the upper floors of which Brady once used, is a far cry from his opulent studio of Civil War days. As the semi-official photographer of Lincoln and other leaders, Brady was a celebrity him-

self. His onetime associate, Alexander Gardner, tells us that the studio was "half baroque palace and half art museum. Elaborate chandeliers, walls covered with mirrors, and the most luxurious furniture provided the setting for other walls closely hung with framed photographs of leaders and celebrities. Some of the pictures were life-size, called 'Imperials'; many were tinted."

In July of 1861 thin-faced, bespectacled, intense Matthew Brady spoke of the motivation which took him to the battlefields when the war began. "I felt I had to go; a spirit in my feet said 'go' and I went!" He started at the Battle of Bull Run, a disaster for both the Union and Brady. The Confederates captured his traveling darkroom wagon, his cameras and supplies. Joining the disorderly rout from the battlefield, he made his way back through Centreville, Fairfax and Bailey's Crossroads to the Long Bridge nearly twenty-five miles away. Arriving at the studio exhausted, he still clung to the one article he'd picked up along the way, a souvenir sword.

He became the world's first war photographer of note, creating a priceless visual record of what the fighting, the leaders, the soldiers and the average citizen looked like. Whenever he could break away from Washington he went to the battles with his famous darkroom wagons. At times when he was needed at the studio he hired other photographers to supplement his coverage of the war.

61

Matthew Brady, an early and great photographer of war. A spirit in his feet said "go" and he "went."

National Archives

People who aspired to prominence sought a sitting with Mr. Brady. Men like President Lincoln and his cabinet members were only too happy to climb the three steep flights to the top floor and the best natural light, and to endure the rigors of having a picture taken. Appointments were scheduled for morning because the light was right then, and postponed if it rained.

21.
The Center Market

Now occupied by the National Archives Building, the former site of the Center Market was at Seventh Street and Pennsylvania Avenue on the south side. Only the street sign, "Market Space," remains as a final echo of its 125-year stay.

The City Market, which moved from Lafayette Square opposite the White House in 1803, relocated at this spot midway between the Capitol and the White House. Its low, open, dingy frame buildings were at the heart of the liveliest quarter of the war-time city. From the market a crowded business district spawned north up Seventh Street, and west along Pennsylvania Avenue and F Streets.

Men did most of the shopping in those days. Important people habitually shopped here carrying shopping baskets. They invariably bowed politely when they met, and sometimes conducted business as they shopped. The market specialized in an abundance of delicacies—venison, wild turkey, ducks, shad and other fish, and succulent seafoods like oysters, crab and terrapin.

The war multiplied the crowds and intensified the activity. When wagon trains passing down Seventh Street met other wagon trains on the Avenue there would occasionally be a traffic jam approximating a riot. The nearby Hay Market and the hack stand on the corner contributed to the uproar. Teamsters, notorious for violent tempers, began shouting; wagons intermingled with riders, hacks, horse cars and pedestrians; all competed in the dust for right-of-way. There were occasional group fist fights, which Washington's police often enjoyed from the safety of the sidewalk while blowing their whistles and awaiting reinforcements.

A jumble of small stores, rooming houses, dozens of saloons, pie and cake places and seedy hotels huddled about the market. As the fighting climbed in intensity in Virginia a growing number of embalming establishments appeared near the Market. Stacks of wooden coffins, upended on the sidewalks, announced their presence. During the unseasonably hot spring of 1864, when Grant's campaign against Richmond was in full

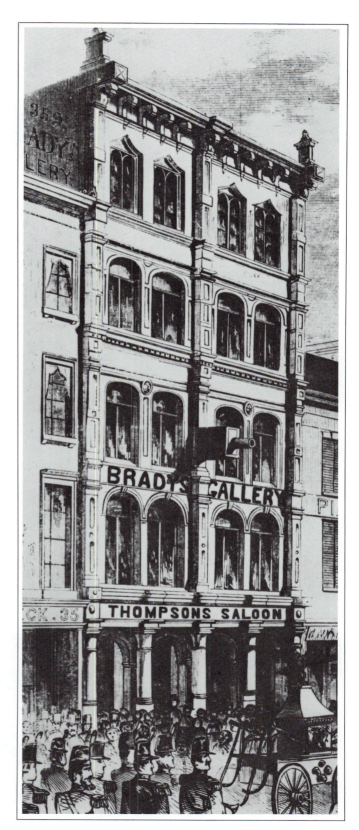

Brady's Photographic Gallery during the Civil War was situated above Thompson's Saloon.
Library of Congress

The shabby old Center Market as it looked about 1865. Slave auctions were held here regularly until 1850. The Market burned down in the 1870's and was replaced by a larger Victorian structure, now also gone. *Library of Congress*

The National Archives Building, present occupant of the site used by the Center Market from 1803 to 1928. *Susan C. Lee*

A striking wartime photograph of Clara Barton by Matthew Brady.

National Archives

course, the city's hospitals and embalming establishments filled to capacity. The citizenry complained. *The Daily Chronicle* stated the matter succinctly, "It insults the meanest animals to have their dead and food in juxtaposition!"

22.
Clara Barton's Rooms

Miss Barton rented rooms at 488½ Seventh Street, just south of the corner of E and Seventh Streets on the east side. The boardinghouse is now gone, replaced by a store.

Many years after the war she owned a large home which can be visited any afternoon except Monday. It is located in the Maryland suburb of Glen Echo overlooking the Potomac at 5801 Oxford Road; the house was designed to resemble a Mississippi River boat. She died here in 1912 at the age of ninety-one.

On September 14, 1862, as a heavy Army wagon topped with white canvas and pulled by a string of mules lurched to a halt at the curb of her Seventh Street lodgings, Miss Barton looked gratefully from her front

On the northeast corner of 7th and D Street to your right stood the photographic studio of Alexander Gardner, one time associate of Matthew Brady. A great photographer too, he took some superb photographs of Mr. Lincoln, among them Lincoln's last likeness, taken four days before his death. *Library of Congress*

stoop and blessed her one friend in officialdom, Major Rucker, Depot Quartermaster of the Army, for the help he had sent her. Eager to be off, she helped load the wagon with the medical stores her friends had sent from Massachusetts and New Jersey. They were the essentials for wounded men—bandages, medicines, lanterns and foods, especially bread, meal, jellies, wine and other liquors. She remembered to wrap a few necessities for herself in a handkerchief and, climbing over the high wagon wheel, she seated herself on the hard wood seat beside the teamster.

The driver cracked his whip; the wagon rumbled forward into perhaps the most exciting story of an American woman in the Civil War. They turned west onto Pennsylvania Avenue. People walking to church dressed in their Sunday best turned to stare at the odd sight. Who had ever seen a woman on a loaded Army wagon, obviously headed for the front? But that woman, a small, thin, determined-looking lady of middle years, knew exactly what she was doing.

She knew a battle was imminent and urged the teamster on toward Harpers Ferry. After passing through Frederick, Maryland, their wagon bogged down behind the miles of Army wagon trains. When the trains stopped at night, Clara bypassed them and followed the artillery directly to Antietam Creek, arriving on the eve of the battle. The next dawn, September 17, she headed toward the rising smoke and roar of heavy fighting on the Union right flank where General Joe Hooker's First Corps had attacked headlong into the divisions of Stonewall Jackson. The battle lines surged back and forth with the utmost ferocity, leaving cornfields, pastures and dirt roads littered with thousands of dead and wounded.

Clara pulled up to a dressing station, already crowded with wounded men, at a farmhouse just behind the artillery positions, and went to work. Even though the Confederate counter-attacks drew fearfully close and the fields filled with the smoke and crash of exploding shells, she stuck to her post.

The Army's medical train lagged far behind, and Clara's supplies were all the doctors had, but they made the vital difference for the mounting numbers of casualties in the farmyard. That night the surgeons used her lanterns to light their operating tables. They used her liquor to deaden the pain. She nursed the wounded, and then cooked for them, using up what food she had and finding more. All her stores were consumed by the time the medical supply wagons pulled up three days later, and she was insensible from exhaustion.

Now, with Army recognition and support, Clara went on to other battles, providing the same life-saving services. In 1882 this indomitable lady led in the founding of the American Red Cross, and became its first president.

An 1846 photograph of the Old Post Office taken the year after Samuel Morse opened the first telegraph office in the country in this building. The wires leading from it are visible above the chimneys. The building is now used by the Tarriff Commission.

Library of Congress

23.
The Old City Post Office

Here, between E and F Streets on Seventh Street's west side, is the same marble building of Civil War days, now used by the Tariff Commission.

By December, 1861, there was deep frustration in the Old Post Office. Behind its marble facade, harassed clerks were up to their green eye-shades in mountains of mail with baffling military addresses. The old practice of publishing the names and addresses of lost mail in the papers was overwhelmed by the sheer volume of undeliverable letters.

Since May the city had been all but upside down. The accommodating southern town of 63,000 natives had been swamped by arriving trains and ships bearing over 150,000 soldiers—and hordes of civilians, too. The military built camps on both sides of the Potomac faster than they could be recorded by old Post Office practices. And it took time to clean up the backlog because the military kept moving. Under the baleful glares of commanders who couched their demands in barracks language, a manful effort was made. The commanders too had to answer to a stern imperative. Next to good food, their lonely boys needed mail from home.

The nerves of the clerks were further frayed by an-

other source of uproar and confusion. The Army had commandeered the cellar of the Post Office as a commissary depot. From early morning until late at night, the streets outside were jammed with wagons and shouting teamsters. The doors banged as officers stamped in and out, submitting requisitions and drawing food for their units. Heavy barrels of coffee, rice, crackers and other staples were rolled up the marble stairs and carted noisily away in commissary wagons; bread was authorized for issue from the bakery in the vaults of the Capitol.

24.
The Patent Office

The old Patent Office is located between F and G Streets on the left (west) side of Seventh Street. It now houses the National Collection of Fine Arts and the National Portrait Gallery.

On the spot where Major L'Enfant, Washington's first city planner, intended to build a national mausoleum and temple for all faiths, the Greek Revival Patent Office stood almost complete in 1861, its south portico a copy of the Parthenon.

Some clerks were suddenly displaced during May of 1861 when Colonel Ambrose Burnside moved his whole First Rhode Island Regiment into the building and bedded them down. They didn't stay long, but other Rhode Island regiments followed. Their hearty, likable commander had already become a marked man, and was later to command the whole Army of the Potomac in its devastating defeat by General Lee at Fredericksburg (December 1862). Today he is perhaps better remembered for his luxuriant side whiskers, called "burnsides," than for his war record.

Like many other public buildings, much of the Patent Office was taken over as an Army hospital. After the Second Battle of Bull Run long rows of wounded men lay on cots in the third floor east salon and galleries. Separating them were rows of high glass cases containing models of curious inventions that had been submitted for patent. Walt Whitman wrote that at night the glass reflected the pale, suffering faces, bandaged limbs, and the watchful doctors and nurses. Pervasive

The Patent Office, built from 1836 to 1867, is one of the city's superb old buildings in the Greek Revival style. It has borne a charmed life, suffering a devestating fire in 1877 which destroyed over 100,000 old patent models. In 1925 it survived an attempt to extend Eight Street directly through it, and again in 1953 President Eisenhower defeated an attempt to demolish it and create a parking lot.
Martin Luther King Library

was the stench of medicines, gangrenous wounds and very sick men.

These same rooms were the joyous scene of President Lincoln's second inaugural ball on the night of March 5, 1865. It was a time of special release, for everyone knew that the long, terrible war was about to end. The wealth, power and beauty of the North gathered here to celebrate. With the music provided by the Finley Hospital Band, the President led the grand march. Mrs. Lincoln followed on the arm of Senator Sumner. A young, lovely lady, Mrs. Marietta Simons remembered sixty years later the pleasure of dancing a square set with her husband, Admiral Farragut, and General Banks.

To those who recalled the sights, sounds and smells of the hospital ward only two years before, the violins, swaying dancers, decorations and elaborate food displays must have seemed a supreme irony.

Mrs. Surratt's boardinghouse. Its 1865 appearance is much the same today except for the front stairway leading to the second floor.

National Archives

25.
Mrs. Surratt's Boardinghouse

Turn right on G Street, go north one block on Sixth Street, then left on H Street. The small old-fashioned brick house a few doors down on the left at 604 H Street was Mrs. Surratt's boardinghouse. Now a Chinese grocery store, this building has a historic and sinister past.

The men who plotted President Lincoln's death met here frequently. Chance led them here, for the chief plotter, John Wilkes Booth, drew Mrs. Surratt's son, John, into the conspiracy. It is one of history's ironic twists that John Surratt, very much a conspirator, escaped overseas and lived a long life. He left his mother to a terrible death.

On April 17, 1865, three days after Lincoln's assassination, the military arrested Mrs. Surratt at her boardinghouse. She was locked up in the Old Capitol Prison and interrogated. Then, removed to the Navy Yard, she was thrust with other suspects into the stifling hold of the Union ironclad, *Saugus,* at anchor in the Anacostia River. At the end of April all the accused were taken to the Arsenal Prison (now demolished). The military trial began May 9 and continued into the sweltering June weather in a vindictive, almost carnival atmosphere.

Found guilty on June 30 and sentenced to hang with three others, Mrs. Surratt turned to the spiritual comfort of her Catholic pastor, Father Jacob Walter of St. Patrick's. The court, meanwhile, had petitioned the new President Johnson for clemency on her behalf. This petition was apparently never received. After much anxious waiting she was hanged in the prison yard of the Arsenal Prison at 1:26 in the afternoon of July 7, 1865.

Doubts would not be stilled. The partisan nature of the trial, and Mrs. Surratt's blameless conduct throughout, bothered the public. Rumors arose of judicial murder. Some felt President Johnson had avoided the chance to pardon her. When Secretary Stanton, stage manager of the trial, died in 1869 his detractors attributed it to his remorse over Mrs. Surratt's execution. There were those who believed Judge Advocate General Holt had purposely blocked the court's clemency petition from reaching the President's desk. When Senator Preston King of New York committed suicide four months after Mrs. Surratt's death, the public was prepared to believe he had punished himself for preventing Miss Anna Surratt, the daughter, from seeing the President with a last minute appeal. The whole ordeal was one of lurid, brutal melodrama, and the innocence or guilt of Mrs. Surratt still escapes us.

Mrs. Surratt before the ordeal of her arrest and trial as a member of the conspiracy to assassinate President Lincoln.

Library of Congress

26.
Headquarters of the Christian Commission

As you travel west on H Street, notice the northeast corner of H and Eighth Streets to your right. This is the site of the Headquarters of the Christian Commission.

Like the Sanitary Commission, No. 4 in the tour above, the Christian Commission labored to help the soldiers, but its purpose was "primarily religious and moral." Only later in the war, as a byproduct, the Commission began to provide for the men's physical care too.

It began in New York November 16, 1861 as an outgrowth of the Christian and humanitarian purposes of the YMCA. An appeal for funds to the farms, towns and cities of the North brought a generous response that continued through the war. Bibles, hymnals, religious tracts and "good" literature were provided for the soldiers without cost. Libraries stocked books in places where there were large numbers of military men—in cities, ships, hospitals. Even "knapsack" books were passed out to soldiers on campaign. The Commission built over two hundred chapels and chapel tents, and delegates held services widely among the field forces and in the hospitals. This effort represented a genuine idealism and religious fervor that had its grassroots throughout the North.

In time food, clothing and hospital stores were also provided. Of special value were diet kitchens set up in general hospitals and convalescent camps. One much appreciated service was the coffee wagons soldiers in the field sometimes found waiting for them at lonely crossroads. This practice the Red Cross continued in later wars.

27.
A Cluster of Hospitals— The City's Northern Rim

Move west on H Street through Eighth and Ninth Streets, a depressed part of the city now being renovated to make room for a new Convention Center. You are passing through what was once a group of Army hospitals that all arose during the single year of 1862 and vanished soon thereafter.

The headquarters of the Christian Commission. Prominent in the picture are the people who dominated the organization—the ministers.

Library of Congress

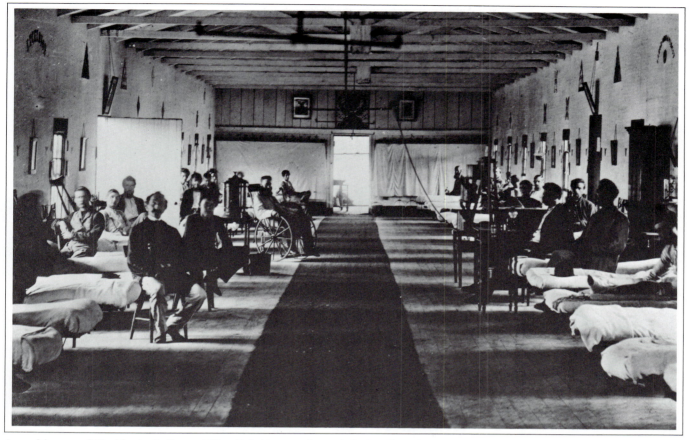

A ward in one of Washington's General Hospitals (Armory Square) during the war.

Junior League of Washington

The costly fighting on the Virginia Peninsula, and the campaigns of the Second Battle of Bull Run and Antietam, filled the city with casualties. At least six makeshift hospitals dotted this quarter. Four were churches—Ascension, Methodist, Presbyterian and St. Patrick's Catholic Church. Two others, the Patent Office and the Ninth Street General Hospital, completed a sprawling temporary group of medical facilities made up mostly of tents clustered in vacant lots about a few brick churches.

As a rule of thumb Massachusetts Avenue was then regarded as the northern rim of the Civil War city. Actually, A. Boschke's Map (1857) shows some built-up areas a few blocks north of this Avenue, but the houses soon gave out and a drab, swampy, cutover landscape took over. It was mostly flat open space, a dumping ground for refuse, with an occasional huddle of barracks or other Army necessities like the Execution Grounds (at present Logan Circle). This plain continued north for about a mile. Then the land climbed abruptly to a shelf seventy or eighty feet above the plain where rolling, wooded and farm lands commanded a spectacular view of the spires of the city and the spreading byways of the Potomac.

The city's prewar wealthy class maintained estates and farms along this shelf. These were commandeered by the arriving Union host in the spring of 1861; the whole shelf from the Anacostia River west beyond Rock Creek was dotted with white tent and hut camps. When the soldiers moved south in the spring of 1862 the doctors took over the best barracks, joined them with tents, and turned them into general hospitals. A row of twelve large hospitals remained here till the end of the war.

Two or three miles north of the hospitals was the city's true frontier, a line of forts on the crest of the low hills that protected the city's northern approaches. Cannon peered through the squat and ugly earthwork walls, and the flag of the Union flew overhead. There was no need to see them to know they were there. The heavy guns practiced constantly. One of the enduring trials of the city's residents was to put up with the continuing roar and racket. It shortened tempers during the day and prevented sleep at night.

MAP 9.

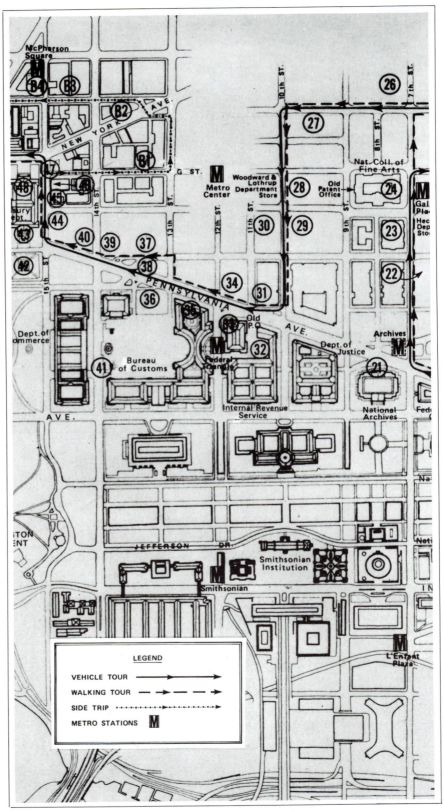

Tenth Street and Central Pennsylvania Avenue.

St. Patrick's Catholic Church, used as an Army hospital during 1862. This church, now gone, faced on F Street near 10th. Today, a Gothic church located on 10th Street between F and G Streets (less than half a block away) replaces the old church.

Dimmock Gallery, George Washington University

TENTH STREET AND CENTRAL PENNSYLVANIA AVENUE

Vehicle Tour —Drive south on Tenth Street to Pennsylvania Avenue, then turn right (northwest) as far as Fifteenth Street; prepare to turn right (north) up Fifteenth Street.

Walking Tour —Walk south on Tenth Street. Turn right on Pennsylvania Avenue, again taking the right side of the street to enjoy the classical buildings of the Federal Triangle.

Services—Walkers joining or leaving the tour in this area could use the METRO CENTER or FEDERAL TRIANGLE STOPS.

You are now in a shopping and business part of the city where commercial parking lots are fairly numerous. Commercial eating places are available on Tenth Street and Pennsylvania Avenue. Also, government cafeterias are located in the buildings of the Federal Triangle south of Pennsylvania Avenue.

28.
St. Patrick's Catholic Church

The present gothic church is to the left on Tenth Street midway between F and G Streets NW. The Church of Civil War days was at the corner of Tenth facing F Street, a few yards to the south of the present one.

From the Eighteenth century to the present day, St. Patrick's has had a valued record of service to the city. In times of danger it became a haven. Around it gathered large numbers of frightened people the entire night of August 24, 1814; not far away, a conquering British Army lit up the city with the flames of burning government buildings. In emergency times it was a hospital during the Civil War.

In early July, 1865, after the war had ended, Father

Jacob Walter, the pastor, received a message from one of his parishioners, Mrs. Mary Surratt. She wished him to come at once to her at the Arsenal Prison where she awaited execution as a conspirator in President Lincoln's murder. He went immediately, but could only be admitted by Colonel Hardy, the prison officer, on condition that he say nothing of her innocence.

He replied, "You wish me to promise that I should say nothing . . . Do you know the relation between a pastor and his flock? I will defend the character of the poorest person in my parish . . . You wish me to seal my lips . . . Of course I cannot let Mrs. Surratt die without the sacraments, so if I must say yes, I say yes!" (Smith, *History of St. Patrick's Church*)

Father Walter was also advised by the authorities to be absent from Mrs. Surratt's execution for his own good. He went anyway to the Arsenal Prison, and stood at her side holding a crucifix which the condemned woman kissed. Then he waited below the gibbet as the trap was sprung.

In 1891 Father Walter broke a 25-year silence about Mrs. Surratt. At the request of Secretary of War Stanton, Father Walter's archbishop had asked him to be silent for this period. The request was tantamount to an order. In 1891 the old man wrote a paper for the Catholic Historical Society, arguing that Mrs. Surratt was innocent.

Brave, troubled Father Jacob Walter—pastor of St. Patrick's Church, the priest who helped Mrs. Surratt in her final hours.

National Archives

As you cross F Street glance to your right at the aging business district. This photograph is of the same street on May 24, 1865. Then a dirt street, it was mostly residential. A Union infantry column, probably a brigade in parade formation, prepares to join its fellows on Pennsylvania Avenue in the final victory parade of the war. The band is in front, and the mounted commanders are in position to march.

National Archives

Contemporary drawing of the Petersen House the night of the assassination, April 14, 1865. The President has been carried inside to a main-floor back bedroom; outside armed soldiers hold the people back from the house. *Library of Congress*

29.
Ford's Theater

Going south on Tenth Street NW past F Street, you see Ford's Theater mid-block on the left.

Here on the evening of April 14, 1865, a Good Friday, Miss Julia Shepherd, a young visitor in town, sat watching the popular comedy, *Our American Cousin.* At odd moments during the second act she penned a note to her father. "The President is in the upper righthand, private box . . . We know Father Abraham is there . . . how sociable it seems, like one family sitting around their parlor fire."

Suddenly the scene changed. A man dropped from the President's box, screamed something at the audience and limped rapidly off the stage past the startled, faltering actors. A piercing yell, then another came

from the box. Someone cried, "He has shot the President!" A few rose to their feet, women clutching their skirts about them as bedlam took over. People climbed onto the stage, jammed the aisles, all shouting and gesturing, shock written on their faces. Most stood in indecision or milled about; then they started pushing slowly toward the doors.

Suddenly soldiers pushed them back to form a corridor through the crowd. Stricken, the people watched the long form of the President borne by soldiers and carried feet first toward the door. Their minds could not accept the drops of blood everyone saw on the stair steps and floor. Someone called to the officer supporting the President's head, asking how serious were the injuries. All were horrified to hear that the wound was mortal.

The next morning Mrs. Lincoln was led, distraught, from her husband's deathbed in the Petersen House. Looking at the dark outline of Ford's Theater across the street, dripping with rain, she cried, "Oh, that dreadful house! That dreadful house!"

After the assassination the Theater was closed, then later used for government purposes. After World War II, Congress had it restored. It is now open to the public as a theater exactly as it appeared that terrible night. The empty, flag-draped box somehow recaptures the atmosphere of the Lincoln presidency and the drama of war years in the city.

30.
The Petersen House

The small brick rowhouse directly across Tenth Street with the plaque on front is the Petersen House. Now restored and furnished, it looks as it did in 1865.

Young Dr. Leale, Army surgeon from Armory Square Hospital across the Mall, had come to Ford's that night especially to see Mr. Lincoln, whom he admired, for the first time. Now he found himself suddenly in charge of the dying President.

Under his direction several soldiers had carried the President from the Theater into Tenth Street, Dr. Leale himself supporting the President's head. As they made their way slowly, Dr. Leale noticed a man waving a candle from a stoop across the street. He told the soldiers to carry the unconscious man to that house. It belonged to Mr. Petersen, the man who had waved the candle.

Meanwhile, Dr. Leale's mind must have absorbed the lurid scene; pine torches stuck in barrels cast a flickering light outside the Theater; angry crowds surged in the muddy street. Someone yelled, "Burn the Theater!" But the soldiers forced order on the mob. Ordered by an officer with a drawn sword, the crowd, cursing and shoving, cleared a path for Dr. Leale's little group.

Once the group was inside the Petersen house, the night-long death watch began. Dr. Leale and the other doctors could do little. Absorbed in caring for the unconscious man, Dr. Leale periodically removed blood clots from the wound with his fingers—to relieve pressure on the brain. Dimly aware of Mrs. Lincoln's occasional hysterical outbursts in the front parlor, he could hear more clearly the urgent voices in the next room as Secretary Stanton's hunt for the assassin got under way. Important people came, stood by the bed a few moments in helpless silence and then left.

Outside, a crowd remained for hours, held back from the house by a cordon of cavalrymen. These were people of the city who cared for the President, and some of them were in tears. The Marquis de Chambrun who came by noticed that many were blacks.

As dawn approached, Dr. Leale realized that the President was dying. He knew from his work with the wounded that men dying of head wounds sometimes regained consciousness a few moments before death. Knowing that Mr. Lincoln's wound would make him blind, and not wishing him to feel alone in his final moments, Dr. Leale held his hand.

But Mr. Lincoln did not regain consciousness. He died at 7:22 on the gloomy morning of April 15, 1865, as a steady drizzle came down outside. Mr. Stanton, at the bedside, broke the heavy silence, "Now he belongs to the Ages."

Ford's Theater today. Open to the public again as a theatre and museum, it has been carefully restored to its appearance the night of Mr. Lincoln's death. To the right of the stage is the empty, flag-draped box.
Susan C. Lee

78

31.
Parade of the Pickpockets— Military Executions

The nearness of the Central Guardhouse (site on the Avenue's south side at about the center of the present Department of Justice Building) sometimes brought a carnival atmosphere to the busy corner of Tenth Street and Pennsylvania Avenue.

Occasionally, a small group of handcuffed pickpockets was brought from the Central Guardhouse to this corner with large placards on their chests announcing their offense. Once a crowd had gathered an Army fifer and drummer would lead the straggling group and its guards up the Avenue sounding the "Rogue's March." Past the White House at Seventeenth Street the procession turned around, accompanied by its tormentors, and made its way back down the Avenue to the Baltimore & Ohio depot. Here they were paraded in front of the cars, then placed aboard and ticketed one way at least as far as Philadelphia.

Large, jeering crowds followed all the way, pressing close and yelling insults. Usually the recipients were overcome by shame, slouching along with averted eyes. Occasionally some bold spirit seemed to enjoy the spectacle of his own ridicule, entering brazenly into the spirit of things. He would march grandly along, head up and bowing comically at his detractors.

On rarer occasions a somber parade also started up the Avenue from this corner. A soldier bound for execution would be brought from the Guardhouse and put in a curtained carriage with a clergyman. Surrounded by a marching column of soldiers, the carriage would pass up the Avenue watched by silent crowds. At Fourteenth Street the procession would turn north, headed for the Execution grounds at what is now Logan Circle.

Executions were sad ceremonial events, designed for their deterrence value. In the center of troops in a hollow square, the condemned would go through the final rituals of spiritual comfort, the reading of the sentence and sometimes a final statement to the assemblage if he chose. One unhappy man, Private Lanahan, called out in a firm voice, "Goodby, Soldiers, goodby." Then he was hanged to the long roll of drums, as the soldiers watched, some of them from nearby Meridian Hill.

There were 266 Union soldiers executed during the war, mostly for murder, mutiny, rape, pillaging and espionage. This compares to one U.S. soldier executed in World War II.

An 1865 photograph of the busy Hay Market, between Ninth and Tenth Streets on the south side of Pennsylvania Avenue (foreground). The building with the tower was the Central Guard House where civilian and soldier offenders were held. Mortician shops clustered along Louisiana Avenue (the diagonal street). The "Canterbury" in the right foreground was a music hall where boisterous and sometimes bawdy acts prevailed—very popular with the public.
Library of Congress

32.
Harvey's Oyster Salon

Between Tenth and Eleventh Streets, Harvey's was a block south of Pennsylvania Avenue on old C Street. This whole area, including C Street, is now taken up by the Internal Revenue Building of the Federal Triangle; the Civil War Harvey's site should be somewhere within the north wing of this classic-style building.

Started in 1858 in an old blacksmith shop, Harvey's became a great success story. Not a chain like McDonald's of today, it was nevertheless a great nineteenth century adventure in fast foods. By mid-1861 the proprietors, the two Harvey brothers, found themselves swamped by customers demanding oysters. Among them was the Army, coming in with orders for 100 to 500 gallons at a time. Oysters had become the fad of the wartime city.

Eighteen to twenty men were kept busy "opening oysters and scalding them in steaming caldrons." As the customers increased, they expanded into a salon 105

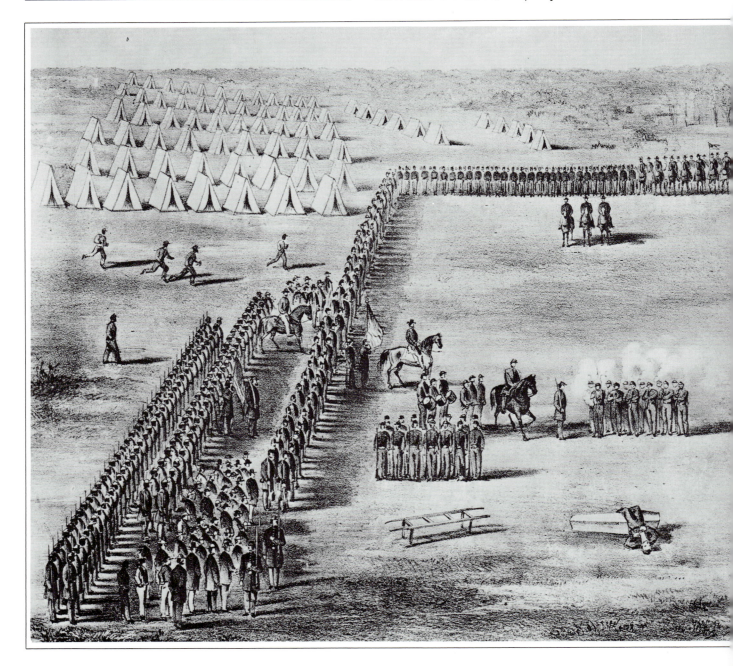

feet long, a record breaker for restaurants of that time. Along one side ran a 100-foot counter, polished and gleaming, where fifty customers at a time were served.

The fall and winter of 1861–62 posed a new problem for the nimble-minded Harveys. Confederate artillery batteries spaced along the Virginia shore of the Potomac shot at all vessels that dared to sail north to Washington. The wharves were lined with idle ships, and oysters became scarce. The Harveys were undeterred. Their ads extolling delicious oysters continued to appear in the papers. Prices were right. Harvey's oyster craft ran the blockade daily in season, regardless of risk,

sometimes with cannon shot splashing nearby. Sometimes a vessel bound for Washington was unlucky. On January 1, 1862, *The Evening Star* reported that the schooner *Mary Willis,* beating her way up the river, had been hit and sunk by rebel guns.

Today, 122 years later, Harvey's carries on, the oldest restaurant in the city. Having moved twice since its early days, it is to be found at 1001 Eighteenth Street NW and also at a new location on Shady Grove Road near Rockville.

33.
The Evening Star
Newspaper Offices

The wartime location of THE EVENING STAR was on the southwest corner of Eleventh Street and Pennsylvania Avenue to the left. This corner no longer exists, as Eleventh Street south of the Avenue was demolished in the late nineteenth century. However, the site of the STAR building is about the east portion of the old Romanesque style post office finished in 1899.

On July 4, 1863, small groups sauntered about the Avenue, after a rather mild Independence Day parade. It was altogether a quiet Fourth of July. Someone noticed a big, flaring placard going up in front of *The Evening Star* office. Bold, large letters announced, "Glorious Victory of The Union Army." A growing, jubilant crowd read on. The Armies of Generals Lee and Meade had fought a great battle at Gettysburg, lasting three days; the southerners had been repulsed. Word travelled fast. Soon there were cheering, roaring crowds moving up the Avenue in impromptu parades, heading for the White House grounds.

The Star was strongly pro-Union. On one occasion in 1861 it reported that a South Carolina newspaper had called President Lincoln a snake. Rising to his defense, *The Star* pointed out that a snake had lots of backbone.

But these were troublesome times even for a pro-Union editor, especially one with a keen nose for news like Mr. W. D. Wallach, brother of the Mayor. In June, 1863, a warrant was issued for his arrest for publishing information on the movements of General Joe Hooker's

This print gives the general aspect of military executions; the troops were paraded in a hollow square with the condemned, clergy, drummers and officials inside—to include the hangman or the firing squad. In this case the unfortunate soldier has just been shot sitting on his coffin.
Library of Congress

army just as the decisive Gettysburg campaign was getting underway—a very touchy time for the Union.

Even today *The Evening Star* of the Civil War years is delightful reading. One of eight newspapers in the city, it provided excellent coverage of the war and political news, then went on to portray the vivid, tumultuous life of a city turned upside-down by the crisis of civil war and an invasion of strangers.

Block print of the Kirkwood House. Vice President Johnson's suite was on the third floor. One of Booth's fellow conspirators, George Atzerodt—a carriage maker, had taken a room directly above the Vice President's suite. He was supposed to knock at Johnson's door at about the same moment (10:15 P.M., April 14, 1865) that Booth was to shoot Mr. Lincoln. When the Vice President opened the door, he would shoot him. Atzerodt lost his nerve, took to drinking and ran away without making the attempt. As a member of the conspiracy he was later hanged anyway.

Martin Luther King Library

34.
The Kirkwood House

This hotel once stood on the northeast corner of Twelfth Street and Pennsylvania Avenue. Torn down after the Civil War, it was replaced by the Raleigh Hotel, one of the city's finest. Sadly enough, it too is now gone; a nondescript office building takes its place.

It was about 7:30 on the somber spring morning of April 15, 1865 with the rain a dismal drizzle, when the carriage of two men pulled up at the Kirkwood House. Senator Sumner, still numb from a night of tragedy, remained in the carriage. General Halleck, Army Chief of Staff, passed the guard detail at the hotel entrance and climbed to the third-floor suite of Andrew Johnson, the Vice President. He told the quiet, self-possessed man that he was now President of the United States. Mr. Lincoln had died a few moments before.

Andrew Johnson, seventeenth President of the United States, was sworn-in at the Kirkwood House the same morning that Abraham Lincoln died.

National Archives

35.
Hooker's Division

At ten o'clock Mr. Johnson stood before Chief Justice Salmon Chase, members of the Lincoln Cabinet and a few friends in the parlor of his suite. With uplifted hand he took the oath of office as the Seventeenth President, then kissed the Bible; "his lips pressed the 21st verse of the 11th Chapter of Ezekiel." "You are President," said Chase, "May God support, guide and bless you in your arduous duties."

So began the four-year ordeal that Mr. Lincoln escaped through death, the almost impossible task of rebuilding the shattered Union. It led in 1867 to President Johnson's impeachment and trial before the Senate. He escaped dismissal from the presidency by a single vote. One hundred and five years later the cry of impeachment was again heard in the land, this time for Richard Nixon.

Look to the left. Most of the area south of Pennsylvania Avenue now occupied by the Federal Triangle, generally between Ninth or Tenth Street and Fifteenth Street, was known as "Hooker's Division" during and after the war. Part of it between Ohio (now gone) and Constitution Avenues along lower Fifteenth and Fourteenth Streets was also called "Murder Bay," possibly the city's worst slum.

The fine lines, ordered columns and Roman porticos of the Federal Triangle are a mocking contrast to the

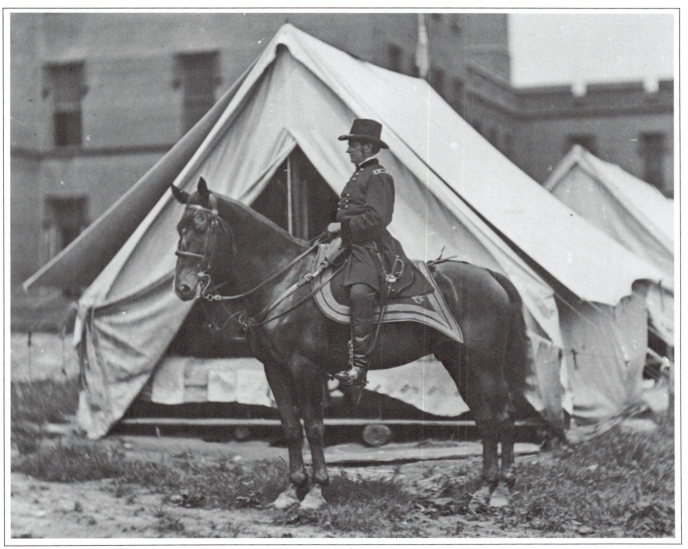

Major General "Fighting Joe" Hooker, one-time commander of the Army of the Potomac, attained a unique kind of immortality by having his name given, for unknown reasons, to Washington's largest gambling and prostitution district (Hooker's Division)—today's Federal Triangle.

National Archives

wartime use of the area. This same piece of real estate, "Hooker's Division," was an entertainment, gambling and red-light district, Washington's largest. Its activities went on in a crowded mass of mostly small frame houses, centers of vice and crime. Along its dimly lighted streets establishments of doubtful reputation flourished. Among them were "Mme. Russell's Bake Oven," "Gentle Annie Lyle's Place," "The Monitor," "Cottage by the Sea" and "Headquarters U.S.A." At one of these places, Nellie Starr's on Ohio Avenue, John Wilkes Booth's mistress, Ella Starr, lived. Her distress was so acute after the President's assassination that she tried to commit suicide.

Part of Hooker's Division today. Gone are the low, ramshackle buildings. Looking south from Pennsylvania Avenue down Twelfth Street, one sees the neo-classical buildings of the Federal Triangle on the right and the old Romanesque Post Office building (built 1899) on the left.
Susan C. Lee

Somehow General Joe Hooker, one-time commander of the Army of the Potomac, had his name given to this quarter. Some say that the camp followers of his division moved in and stayed here when his troops went south by riverboat to the fighting in the spring of 1862. Whatever the reason, the name stuck—and then some. At least one historian has surmised that the term hooker, now defined as a prostitute, could have found its origin in these streets, not half a mile from the White House.

Gamblers, criminals, deserters, pickpockets, prostitutes, flimflam artists and others who wanted to get rich quick by fleecing the soldiers gathered here. The latter flocked into the area in the evenings, looking for excitement and adventure. *The Evening Star* carried

running tongue-in-cheek commentaries on the daily happenings: a soldier is knocked "flat-horizontal" on Ohio Avenue; soldiers riot outside Miss Margaret Veneble's place, smashing windows and disturbing the girls; a prankster blows a whistle on one corner, bringing the police to protect their own—then he goes to another corner and repeats . . . after two hours he is finally run down by exasperated police; a lady of "the fancy class" was "drunk, disorderly, profane, indecent and outrageous" on lower Thirteenth Street—since she wouldn't give her name to police she was sent to the workhouse under the name "Mary Drunk." This and much, much more!

The Provost Marshal's patrols and police worked at the uphill battle of keeping order. But even the former had lapses. *The Evening Star* complained that their horses were sometimes seen hitched to the rail outside some of the fanciest establishments.

36.
The Old Prescott House

This small hotel was located near the southwest corner of Thirteenth Street and Pennsylvania Avenue. Now the site is an empty space just east of the District of Columbia building. The place deserves notice for it was a wartime political prison and recalls the prolonged attack made on the civil liberties of American citizens throughout the Civil War.

Washington, indeed the whole North, contained thousands of active southern sympathizers, as well as many loyal citizens who opposed the war firmly for Constitutional and other reasons. With the Union beset on all sides and barely afloat in the early, perilous days of the war, President Lincoln felt compelled to make the difficult decision on April 27, 1861 to suspend writs of *habeas corpus* in the vicinity of the military line between Washington and Philadelphia. American citizens could be arrested by military authorities and jailed indefinitely without charges or a trial. Later this geographic area was enlarged to include the whole North, and Congress, in 1863, backed the President up.

A note was enough to jail a man: "Arrest man referred to in your letter of the 11th and send him to . . ." Signed, Simon Cameron, Secretary of War. Another member of the Cabinet, Secretary Seward, is supposed to have said to the British Minister, "My Lord, I can touch a bell at my right hand and order the arrest of a citizen of Ohio. I can touch the bell again and order the imprisonment of a citizen of New York . . . Can the Queen of England do so much?"

Prison commanders of places like the Old Prescott House were directed "to refuse to allow themselves to be served with writs, and if service had been secured, either to decline to appear, or to appear and courteously refuse to carry out the instruction of the court." The records of the Federal Commissary General of Prisons revealed that more than 13,000 Americans were imprisoned by the military between 1862 and 1865 throughout the North. This figure is probably on the low side.

37.
Grover's National Theater

Located near the junction of E Street and Pennsylvania Avenue, midway between Thirteenth and Fourteenth Streets on the right (north) is today's "National," the latest of five theaters that have stood on this same spot; the earlier four were destroyed by fire.

About eleven P.M. on a mild fall evening in 1862, Mr. Leonard Grover was feeling somewhat nervous as the performance at his National Theater came to an end. The time was shortly after the issuance of the Emancipation Proclamation, and the feeling against President Lincoln was running high among some of the city's southerners. The President, Vice President and their wives were in the audience. When the play ended, both courtesy and caution led Mr. Grover to precede the dignitaries to their carriage.

Outside, he found that the carriage driver was drunk and surrounded by a jeering, jostling crowd; these were the makings of trouble. The presidential party had paused in dismay at the door, but Grover quickly ushered them into the carriage, climbed into the driver's seat and seized the reins. Before the crowd could realize what had happened, he drove away at a smart trot and delivered his distinguished passengers himself to their homes. At the door of the White House, the Lincolns each took hold of one of Mr. Grover's hands in parting;

Bringing in the Misses Scott as prisoners to Fall's Church, Virginia. Political prisoners like these were sometimes taken to places like the old Prescott House where they were frequently held for long periods without trial.
Martin Luther King Library

The wartime appearance of Mr. Grover's National Theater. Flanking it on both sides was "Rum Row," a collection of saloons. The current National Theater, a Washington Institution since the 1830's, is scheduled for rebuilding as a part of the modernization of Pennsylvania Avenue.

The National Theater, Washington

the President declared, "Mr. Grover, you have done me a great service tonight and one I shall never forget."

Mr. Lincoln attended the National Theater at least a hundred times during his presidency, sometimes with his wife and official parties, and often with his son Tad, who loved the theater. At times he went alone, and on many of these occasions he invited Mr. Grover to sit with him in his box. Mr. Grover believed that attending the theater was one of Mr. Lincoln's escapes from the cares and pressures of the White House. Tad was at the National the evening his father was killed a few blocks away at Ford's Theater.

38.
Foreshadowing of a Murder

Before you leave the National Theater, pause for a moment and notice the area directly in front of the theater.

On April 14, 1865, at about 4:00 P.M., a little more than six hours before President Lincoln was to meet up with his assassin, John Wilkes Booth dismounted from

A print of the times expressing the nation's horror of John Wilkes Booth after the Lincoln assassination.

Library of Congress

his horse here and shook hands with an actor friend, John Matthews. They were standing on the Avenue's north side near the tip of a small triangle in front of the theater (which is a casualty of the Avenue's current restoration). "Have you seen Lee's officers just brought in?" queried Matthews, gesturing toward a group of ragged prisoners moving by. "Yes, Johnny, I have," said Booth. Then mounting his horse, he struck his hand against his forehead, "Great God! I have no longer a country!"

Booth then asked Matthews for a favor—to carry a note to the editor of *The National Intelligencer,* because he might be leaving town that evening. Matthews agreed and put the letter in his pocket.

That evening, when Matthews heard of the assassination, and rumors that Booth was the assassin, he remembered the letter, still in his pocket. He couldn't recall later how he arrived at his hotel, but locking the door in haste, he read the letter. It contained Booth's justification to the public for killing the President. He burned the letter in the grate of his fireplace.

39.
Newspaper Row

At the corner of Fourteenth Street and Pennsylvania Avenue, look north (right) at the first block of Fourteenth Street on the east side.

Low, shabby buildings, long gone, occupied this site. During the war these were known as Newspaper Row. The one-block-long neighborhood suddenly mushroomed in 1861 into the largest center of political and war news in North America. An incredible change had come to sleepy, complacent Washington.

About sixty important, out-of-town newspapers set up bureaus on this block. Working in, or passing through, Newspaper Row during the war was a colorful colony of resourceful newsmen and war artists. They waged an unequal, running battle against the

Newspaper Row during the Civil War. Notice the Ebbitt House, a fine Washington Hotel, on the F Street corner and the bureaus of the leading newspapers of the day—the *New York Herald, New York Tribune World, Boston Advertiser, New York Times, Western Union,* **etc.**

Martin Luther King Library

Julia Ward Howe, who wrote "Battle Hymn of the Republic" early one morning at Willard's.

Federal Censor who operated out of a room at the National Hotel. Their gathering place was across the street at Willard's Hotel in the reception rooms, corridors and bars. There they talked, drank and ferreted out the news.

Among those who could be seen at Willard's in the war's early months was the correspondent of *The London Times,* "Bull Run" Russell. Trained in the Crimea and India, he had a critical eye for the undisciplined Union volunteers in the early days of 1861. His accurate, pungent copy was unpopular reading among Union politicians and soldiers not yet able to face the brutal realities of civil war. He was the first of that adventurous breed, the modern war correspondent.

Newspaper Row lives on, an example of continuity in a changing city. At the northern end of this same block is the National Press Building, the nation's national and international news center today.

40.
Willard's Hotel

To the right, on the northwest corner of Fourteenth Street and Pennsylvania Avenue, is today's Willard's, successor to the Civil War Willard's that stood on the same corner.

Willard's had long been a gathering place for those who favored the Union. During the war it became the very nerve center of the North. Everyone of consequence came here. Its bars, sitting rooms, corridors and dining rooms swarmed from morning to night with politicians, lobbyists, financiers, contractors, officers, war correspondents—anyone who wished to see or be seen, become informed, visit, make contacts, use influ-

Willard's Hotel in the '60's. More than the Capitol itself Willard's was the heart of the Union, for here Northern leaders from all over the country gathered throughout the war.

From the balcony on the second floor, Mr. Lincoln and General Burnside watched the Ninth Union Corps (some 30,000 men) march down Fourteenth Street past Willard's into Virginia. They were joining General Grant's Army for its attack into the Wilderness (May, 1864). With all the noise, crowds and excitement Walt Whitman thought few of the marching men realized that they were under the eye of the President.

Library of Congress

ence, make deals or eat and drink. It goes without saying that Lincoln and Grant stayed here their first nights in the city.

After the First Battle of Bull Run, when thousands of leaderless, beaten soldiers milled about outside in the streets, Walt Whitman was outraged to see "shoulder straps" (officers) crowding Willard's. "Where are your men?" He wrote, "Sneak, blow, put on airs in Willard's sumptuous parlors and barrooms. Bull Run's your work!"

Here early one November morning in 1861, Julia Ward Howe wrote "The Battle Hymn of the Republic." On the way back from a large military review at Bailey's Crossroads, a few miles southwest of the city, her carriage moved through long columns of blue-clad troops singing "John Brown's Body," as they marched back to their camps on Arlington Heights. Her companion and friend, Reverend James Clarke, suggested that she could write more fitting words to such a fine tune.

She retired that night with the stirring melody ringing in her ears. Rising before dawn the next morning, she quickly jotted down the verses as she sat at a small table in her room and then went back to bed. Mrs. Howe's great war hymn had captured the North's deepest convictions about the war—a majestic call to arms to save the Union and erase slavery from the land.

41.
Murder Bay

A block or so south of Pennsylvania Avenue, mostly between Thirteenth and Fifteenth Streets, was the notorious slum, Murder Bay. Where the southern half of the Commerce Department and the Bureau of Customs buildings now stand, this enclave of disease and poverty bordered to the west on the Ellipse just southeast of the White House.

Across Pennsylvania Avenue (south side) from Willard's Hotel stood the most feared address in the Union, 217 Pennsylvania Avenue—a two story brick building. It was the Headquarters of the War Department Secret Service; its chief was ruthless General Lafayette C. Baker, a man of restless, driving energy, who packed hundreds of men and women into Federal prisons without trial.
Library of Congress

Murder Bay was probably the worst slum of the wartime city. By late 1861 the blacks from Maryland and parts of Virginia believed that if they escaped their masters a haven could be found in Washington. At first they came in small groups; after the Emancipation Proclamation (September 1862) the stream became a flood. Contrabands, they were called, and arriving with nothing but the ragged clothing on their backs, they crowded into Murder Bay and other slums about the city. Black shanty towns sprang up near the forts, and by 1865 about 40,000 blacks had come to the city.

They crossed the bridges with jubilant hearts and songs of praise for Massa Lincoln, free at last, but destined for the cruelest disillusionment. Thousands settled at Murder Bay, crowding into shacks, lean-tos and alleys, where disease soon found them. The city's already meager services were overwhelmed by the wartime explosion of population. Charitable institutions, concerned private citizens, the Military Governor and the Army Quartermaster Corps all worked to ease the suffering. But they were untrained in coping with social problems of this magnitude. Nor did the blacks have the skills for caring for themselves in the competitive society of city life. Many blacks died, neglected and in dire poverty. Some of these Freedmen's graves can be found today in Arlington National Cemetery, in the oldest, northeast part.

General William T. Sherman as he looked during his campaign against Atlanta and his march to the sea. *National Archives*

42.
The General Sherman Monument

As you approach the right (north) turn from Pennsylvania Avenue into Fifteenth Street, note the mounted statue of General William T. Sherman, the first Union Commander after Grant, in the small green park to your left. The serenity of the scene, a little apart from the busy street, contrasts strikingly with the powerful, irascible nature of "Uncle Billy." He was a born fighter.

Early in the war, newspapermen reported that Sherman was crazy. Short on tact, and poor at public relations, he was good at what counted in a soldier. Like General Patton of a later war, he knew how to make the moves that got his Army forward. On the road to Atlanta he habitually found and engaged the Southern Army and then pivoted around it on one flank or the other, forcing its retreat. Through this flanking tactic, and others like it, he husbanded his own men and animals.

He was bold. His army seemed always on the move. After taking Atlanta, he simply cut supply and telegraph lines to the North and disappeared into central Georgia, his 68,000 men living off the land. The first news the North had of him was a telegram five weeks later on December 23, 1864 presenting captured Savannah to President Lincoln as a Christmas president. His army had cut a wide swath of devastation completely across Georgia. He defended this destruction on the grounds that he had shortened a terrible war by destroying the South's final "breadbasket."

Although generally disliked by southerners, General Sherman had strong sympathies for the South. When General Joseph E. Johnston's Southern Army surrendered to him near Raleigh, North Carolina, on April 17, 1865 he gave them generous terms. Time and events worked against him, however—Lincoln had been killed three days earlier, and power had fallen to War Secretary Stanton and the Republican radicals in the Senate. They wished to punish the South and scornfully repudiated Sherman's peace terms.

Uncle Billy was not a forgiving man. The following month he met Secretary Stanton in the reviewing stand at the Union victory parade in Washington. As his Army passed in front of the White House, General Sherman abruptly refused Stanton's offered hand.

Site of Murder Bay, perhaps the city's worst slum. The buildings of the Federal Triangle shown here, the Commerce Department and Bureau of Customs, occupy the site.
Susan C. Lee

MAP 10.

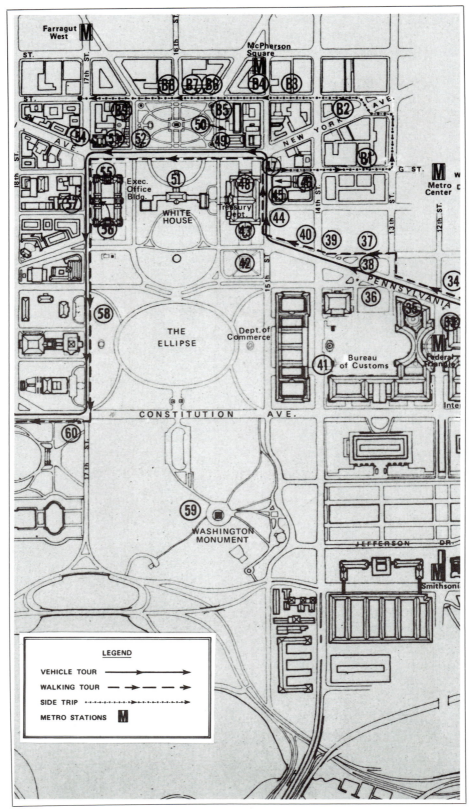

Fifteenth Street and Upper Pennsylvania Avenue.

The Treasury Building as fort and barracks, the city's last-ditch stronghold if attacked by the Virginians in the Spring of 1861. Notice the stacked sandbags on the South Portico and the Zouave uniforms of the Fifth Massachusetts Regiment who camped here. This exotic uniform with floppy, red pantaloons, loose, short jackets and fez caps was thought very glamorous and copied from the French Army.

Martin Luther King Library

FIFTEENTH STREET AND UPPER PENNSYLVANIA AVENUE

Vehicle Tour—Turn right (north) on Fifteenth Street; drive about a quarter of a mile up Fifteenth Street, then take the first left turn which places you on upper Pennsylvania Avenue heading west. Go three blocks, passing the White House on your left, and prepare to turn left (south) on Seventeenth Street.

Walking Tour—Turn right and walk north on Fifteenth Street. After passing F and G Streets, turn left at the light and cross Fifteenth Street to the south sidewalk of upper Pennsylvania Avenue. Walk past the White House on your left to Seventeenth Street; prepare to turn left onto Seventeenth Street.

Services—Walkers joining or leaving the tour near Fifteenth and lower Pennsylvania Avenue could use the METRO CENTER or the FEDERAL TRIANGLE METRO STOPS. Those arriving or leaving the tour near the White House area could best use the MC PHERSON SQUARE or FARRAGUT WEST METRO STOPS.

Commercial parking lots are located near the tour route, but this is an active government, business and banking center, and sometimes the lots are full.

Some of the finest places to lunch in the city are found near the upper Pennsylvania Avenue tour route, particularly near Seventeenth Street.

43.
The Treasury Building

Turning right from Pennsylvania Avenue onto Fifteenth Street, the Greek Revival bulk of the Treasury looms on the left.

Notice how the location blocks a view of the White House from Pennsylvania Avenue. Supposedly impatient with the delays of a stiff-necked Congress, President Andrew Jackson is said to have pounded his cane into the ground and ordered, "Put it here!" Actually, this is the third Treasury building to be built on the same general site. The British burned the first in 1814, and the second one burned of its own accord in 1833. Still under construction, but usable, in 1861, the third Treasury is the one we see today.

In April 1861, with the menacing new Confederacy springing up all around isolated Washington, General Winfield Scott, aged commander of the tiny U.S. Army, planned a last ditch defense of the capital city. He had only a few Regular troops. In case of attack, he decided that the new Treasury building, solidly built of sandstone, stocked with food and with a deep well in the basement, could become the city's last stronghold. When other makeshift forts, the Capitol, City Hall and the Patent Office were abandoned under attack, the soldiers were to retreat to the Treasury. The President and the Cabinet would be brought into the building. Then the Treasury would hold out until help came from the North. This drastic plan of defense was never used.

On the afternoon of August 30, 1862, worried citizens gathered around the bulletin board posted at the Treasury waiting for news of the front. They had endured the day before the uninterrupted roar of massed artillery fire; today it began again, reverberating through the sultry, heavy air. A bulletin was posted, "Great victory!" But over 10,000 dead and wounded lay scattered about the same Bull Run battlefield of a year ago. Surgeons and nurses were ordered to report at 5:00 p.m. to the Maryland Avenue rail depot.

Next morning came disappointment. The casualty reports were true, but the arriving wounded told a story of terrible losses and staggering defeat. To Hay, his secretary, the President succinctly summed up the defeat. "Well, John, we are whipped again."

Women clerks leaving the Treasury on a rainy afternoon in 1865. When the war began there were only a tiny number of women working in Washington, among them Clara Barton. Four years later (1865) women had established a foothold in government employment; 500 worked at the Treasury and 100 more at the Interior Department. The pay was $500 to $900 a year.

Martin Luther King Library

The next afternoon the ominous artillery fire resumed. Stonewall Jackson was pounding at the very gates of Washington as he furiously attacked the shaken Federals at nearby Chantilly, now near Dulles Airport; his apparently invincible troops charged repeatedly through the sheets of rain of a violent thunderstorm. The frightened Union boys held him "by a hair," their commander dead on the field. On the Union's darkest day the people of the city felt the United States was staggering toward total and inevitable collapse.

44.
Where Walt Whitman Worked

Glance to the right at the southeast corner of Fifteenth and F Streets, today's location of the Washington Hotel. Here stood the Corcoran Building, a red brick five-story structure, tall for buildings of that time. It was the Pay Department of the Military Department of Washington.

Walt Whitman worked here two or three hours a day to make ends meet and to be able to buy small gifts of food, candy, soft drinks and writing materials for the men in the hospitals. He copied pay documents by hand in Major Hapgood's fifth floor office. The rest of the time he did as he pleased, sometimes drafting news columns for a New York paper and writing letters, but most often visiting the soldiers in the hospitals.

He liked the high vantage point of Major Hapgood's office. Looking south he could see far down the broad Potomac, "a noble river," and the lovely, wooded hills of Arlington as well.

Whitman couldn't help noticing that many convalescent and crippled soldiers, some in the light blue uniform of the Invalid Corps, had to climb the five stories to Major Hapgood's office to receive their pay. Some on crutches, some with canes, they made their way slowly up the steep stairs, resting pale and winded on the landings. They arrived "very weary and faint" at Major Hapgood's office where, sad to say, the pay of more than a few was withheld because of technicalities and red tape. He remembered they looked "so disappointed."

A famous corner but hard to recognize—looking up Fifteenth Street from Pennsylvania Avenue. The Treasury, unseen, is just to the left, and the back of the Corcoran building (now replaced by the Washington Hotel) is at center. Walt Whitman worked on the back, top floor in this building. From one of the three windows shown here he liked to look down at the Potomac River and the wooded Virginia shoreline. The cannon shown is a '15 Rodman, the largest of the whole fort system. There were only two of them. *Library of Congress*

45.
Rhodes Tavern

Rhodes Tavern is on the northeast corner of Fifteenth and F Streets, across from the Treasury Building.

This worn gray building, a third of its former size, is the oldest commercial structure in the city. Its foundations were laid in 1799, the year of George Washington's death. It was at one time or another a tavern, an early community center, the polling place in the District for the first city election, a court house and a bank. Now, real estate developers threaten to tear it down.

Before 1850 the building served for a time as a tavern. Slave dealers met here and conducted business over their meals. By coincidence, just across Fifteenth Street in Room 18 of the Treasury, the last slave owners in the District of Columbia were paid compensation on January 1, 1863 for their freed slaves. Congress had voted to free them on April 16, 1862. Former slaveholders in the city lined up at the cashier's window to receive slightly less than a million dollars as recompense for the loss of 2,989 slaves. This was the only case of compensated emancipation in the United States. The average compensation per slave was $300; the highest allowed was $788.

The city played a scandalous role in the slave trade before it was stopped in 1850. When the tobacco lands of Virginia and Maryland were exhausted from overplanting during the first half of the nineteenth century, hard-pressed plantation owners sold off their slaves to dealers in the city. They were then resold to work the cotton plantations of the deep south. An outraged Senator John Randolph of Virginia attacked the notorious trade before the ante-bellum Senate. "In no part of Africa, not even excepting the rivers on the coast of Africa, was there so great, so infamous a slave market, as in . . . the seat of government . . . which prides itself on freedom."

46.
Jay Cooke and Company

The First National Bank of Washington was Jay Cooke's subsidiary bank in Washington. It stood near the F Street corner at 452 Fifteenth Street.

One cold day in January 1862, President Lincoln huddled close to General Montgomery Meig's stove in his Quartermaster-General's office at Union Army Headquarters. "What shall I do?" he wondered out loud, "Chase (Secretary of the Treasury) has no money, and he tells me he can raise no more . . . the bottom is out of the tub!"

Rhodes Tavern today in disrepair and on the verge of demolition.
Susan C. Lee

A large part of the solution arrived shortly in the person of Jay Cooke, a Philadelphia banker whose beard and appearance gave him the benign look of one of the apostles. Unlike them he had a keen nose for money, a passion for doing things big, and advertising skills unique for his time. Opening offices across the street from the Treasury in early 1862, he was appointed a special Treasury agent.

With his brother heading his Washington interests, Cooke immersed himself in the task of selling a $500,000,000 bond issue with a six percent return to the public. He sold bonds like hotcakes, for Cooke was a new breed of banker the likes of which the North had never seen. His approach at bond sales offices throughout the country was a drum-fire, hard-sell patriotic appeal and just plain razzle-dazzle. Selling the entire issue and $13,000,000 more by January, 1864, he earned a commission of $1,750,000.

The Union's financial success which he did so much to win was fully as important as great victories in battle, for meanwhile the finances of the Confederate government were growing steadily more chaotic.

47.
G Street

G Street intersects Fifteenth Street from the right (east) as you pass the long, pillared Treasury Building to the left (west).

The morning of April 15, 1865, was heavy and gloomy with drizzle turning into slanting rain. A little after 9:00 A.M. Noah Brooks, a news correspondent from California, hurried east on G Street toward Ford's Theater. He had heard the rumors but wanted to find out for himself what had happened the night before. Groups of people gathered along G Street in the rain. The President had died at the Petersen House. Brooks heard the churchbells beginning to toll and the cannon in the distant forts begin to fire their measured tribute.

He noticed a group of bareheaded officers marching toward him. Behind them was the flag-draped coffin of President Lincoln, carried by soldiers. Then followed a small cavalry escort, under arms. As the small cortege passed on its way to Fifteenth Street, and then to the White House, all bystanders stood silently, their hats in their hands. The only sound was the steady tramp of the soldiers on the dirt street.

Seen from the north, the small wartime State Department building is dwarfed by the mass of the Treasury just to the south. The former was demolished in 1866 to make way for the north front of the Treasury.

Library of Congress

48.
The Old State Department

The small, brick, wartime State Department stood on the south-west corner of Fifteenth Street and upper Pennsylvania Avenue. It stood on the same site as the first State Department in the city, burned by the British in 1814. Soon after the Civil War, this building too disappeared to make way for the present north wing of the Treasury.

Since most of the dramatic decision-making on the war took place in the military departments, it would have been understandable if the urbane, smiling Mr. William H. Seward, Secretary of State, were upstaged by his cabinet colleagues in the War and Navy Departments. Just the reverse was true. He more than held his own among the Cabinet members, and probably was first among them. Why? Because if Lincoln could afford to trust anyone, he could trust Seward.

In those days of angry, bitter side-taking which split country, family and friends, the affable Seward had a talent for guarding his tongue and getting along with people. His detractors charged that he was two-faced; even the fair-minded Navy Secretary, Gideon Welles, had few good words to say of him in his diary. But many felt the man possessed discretion and integrity.

Of great value to Lincoln was Mr. Seward's good judgment. He seemed more open-minded, less willing to condemn, more willing to appraise the alternatives, and, generally, to come down on the side of moderation. This possibly was the central tie between the two men, since Lincoln was permanently caught between factions demanding extreme solutions. Lincoln further recognized Mr. Seward's deep disappointment at not being the Republican candidate for President, himself, in 1860. And he must have appreciated that Seward bore him no grudge. Indeed, Seward had long since written his wife that "the President is the best of us."

In early April 1865, Mr. Seward was painfully injured in a fall from his carriage. Returning from captured Richmond, the President hurried to Seward's sickbed. Noticing that his head bandages interfered with his hearing, Lincoln stretched his lanky form out on the bed beside the injured man and spoke in his ear the momentous news of approaching peace.

It was the last time Seward was ever to see him. Five days later the President had been assassinated, and Seward himself lay close to death from an assassin's attempt that same night. The weakened Secretary was not told of Lincoln's death. A week or so after the tragic event the sick man happened to notice from his bed a flag flying at half mast over the War Department. "The

President is dead," he said. "If he had been alive he would have been the first to call on me, but he has not been here, nor has he sent to know how I am, and there is the flag at half mast." Tears ran down his cheeks.

Brady photograph of William H. Seward, Lincoln's Secretary of State. He stayed on in President Johnson's cabinet to accomplish the purchase of Alaska from Imperial Russia in 1867.

National Archives

49.
Headquarters Defenses of Washington

The location of this brick house was on the northeast corner of Pennsylvania Avenue and Madison Place. Today the columned Treasury Annex occupies this site to the right (north) of Pennsylvania Avenue.

At the hour of sunset on September 1, 1862, all over the city people took shelter in doorways to escape the violent downpour, and heard, interspersed with cracks of thunder, the sounds of heavy fighting at Chantilly (near today's Dulles Airport). Everyone sensed that the Union Army was taking another whipping.

That night a sleepless, discouraged President had decided to change horses in mid-stream and dismiss General John Pope, the beaten Union commander. Early next morning he placed General George McClellan in command of the city and the exhausted troops falling back on it. In the afternoon he explained to an incredulous Cabinet, united only in their distrust of McClellan, that the "Army was tumbling into Washington" and there was no one else the Army trusted.

Look directly across Pennsylvania Avenue from the north front of the Treasury. Here this elegant building once stood on the northwest corner of Fifteenth and Pennsylvania Avenue, from 1824 to 1904. Built by George Hadfield, architect of the Lee Mansion, it was used as a branch bank of the United States, then (1845) the location of Riggs Bank to this day. President Lincoln deposited his salary at Riggs throughout the war in a checking account.
Martin Luther King Library

The General moved with speed and decision. He chose this building as his headquarters and it became a center of furious activity. He himself rode far out the Fairfax road to meet the retreating forces, badly mauled, but still intact. When the tired regiments recognized him, the men broke ranks and crowded round, cheering for "Little Mac" to lead them back into battle.

Within the safety of Washington's forts confusion gave way to order; the whole Army moved into camps; troops were fed and rested. New regiments arrived daily from the north. Cavalry patrols swept the city of strag-

glers and skulkers. In short, it was a miracle of recovery with the hub of it all McClellan's busy headquarters on Pennsylvania Avenue.

Three days later strong Federal advance forces pushed north in search of Lee's Army which had crossed into Maryland. Within a week the restored Union Army, 87,000 strong, followed. They crossed all the city bridges from Arlington, jamming the streets with marching, dusty blue columns. Hours later the Army, with its trains and animals, had vanished to the north on the roads leading into western Maryland.

Waiting at his headquarters for orders that never came from Mr. Lincoln, General McClellan finally mounted up and, on his own initiative, followed his Army. Within two weeks, on September 17, 1862, the Blue and Gray armies had met in the rolling countryside near Sharpsburg, Maryland to fight again. Back in the city "Little Mac's" headquarters at Madison Place continued to control the city forts and the 70,000 men left to defend the capital.

50.
The Seward Home

To the right (north) off Pennsylvania Avenue, about forty-five feet along Madison Place, is the site of the brick mansion that was the home of Secretary of State William H. Seward. The red brick Court of Claims occupies the site today.

On the evening of April 14, 1865, near ten o'clock, the Seward family was about to retire. Mr. Seward, badly injured in a fall from his carriage, was resting in his third-floor bedroom. A tall, powerfully built young man arrived at the front door and declared that he wished to personally deliver some medicine to the Secretary. Despite qualms, the servant led him up the stairs. Seward's son, Frederick, becoming suspicious, began to question the man. A moment later he fell to the floor, lacerations on his face. His assailant then stabbed a male nurse, and rushed into Mr. Seward's bedroom. Hurling Fanny Seward, a daughter, to the floor, he leaned over the bed, stabbing and slashing at the startled Secretary. Mr. Seward, partially shielded by his bandages, was thrown to the floor behind his bed, gravely wounded.

The attacker, thinking he had killed Mr. Seward, rushed back down the stairs, wounding a State Department messenger en route. He ran through the door chased by a family servant crying out in vain for help to arrest him.

The would-be assassin was Lewis Paine, a member of

Booth's band of conspirators. While Paine was attacking Seward at home, Booth was shooting President Lincoln at Ford's Theater. Thus began for the city a night of alarm and confusion; people feared a plot to destroy the entire government.

Paine was arrested a few days later, at Mrs. Surratt's house, after he emerged from his hiding place in a tomb at Congressional Cemetery. Three months later, on July 9, 1865, he and three other conspirators were hanged in the yard of the Federal Prison at the Arsenal.

This is probably a picture of the building used as the Headquarters Defenses of Washington on the northeast corner of Pennsylvania Avenue and Madison Place. The scene is of General Sherman's "bummers", folk who had attached themselves to his Army during the march across Georgia. As a contrast to the "spit and polish" of the Army of the Potomac, Sherman decided that all Washington should see his Army as it really was—to include hordes of campfollowers. They made a colorful and unforgettable sight as they passed up Pennsylvania Avenue in rear of each army corps.

Junior League of Washington

The Seward home on Madison Place, known for the misfortunes which befell its occupants.

President Lincoln reviewing a number of New York regiments on July 4, 1861.

National Archives

51.
The White House

To your left, one block from Fifteenth Street, sits the White House, the most famous home in America.

Life here had some special drawbacks. During the Civil War blueclad sentries paced about the place, an interference with the family's privacy. Until 1859, the White House sewage emptied directly into the Ellipse. Gas-lit since 1848, the White House acquired city water only two years before the Lincolns moved in. The marshy Ellipse sloped down to the Potomac. Here the junction of the malodorous city canal with the river near the stump of the Washington Monument, the proximity of the city dump at the bottom of Seventeenth Street, and the nearness of Murder Bay to the east all combined to make the White House an unhealthy place. The Lincolns' son Willie died of typhoid fever, and Lincoln himself contracted small pox while President.

Although the Lincolns were the official leaders of Washington society, neither was naturally suited to the task, though both worked at it. Mrs. Lincoln was deeply troubled by personal insecurities and anxieties. She was quick to take offense at innocent remarks. The President was usually distracted, often fatigued, and preferred informal gatherings. Whitman remembered him at a White House reception "dressed all in black with white kid gloves and clawhammer coat . . . shaking hands, looking very disconsolate and as if he would give anything to be somewhere else."

There was much bad news; disaster followed disaster until late in the war. One evening in early 1863 Lincoln entered a room where Mrs. Keckley, the housekeeper, was at work fitting Mrs. Lincoln's dress. He was agitated. His wife asked, "Where have you been, Father?" "To the War Department," he answered. "Any news?" "Yes," he replied in a low voice, "Plenty of news, but no good news. It is dark, dark everywhere."

There was occasionally good news. Colonel Eckert took the word of General Thomas' victory at Nashville on December 16, 1864 to the White House late at night. He remembered the President standing at the head of the stairs, lanky and gaunt in his nightshirt, his form lit by the ghostly illumination of the candle in his hand. Mr. Lincoln smiled his thanks and retired.

An artist's conception of a reception in the East Room of the White House late in the war. Included are good likenesses of nearly everyone of official prominence in Washington at that time.

National Archives →

A big moment in the Union Victory Parade, May 24, 1865. Some 200,000 Union combat troops in two days passed in review before President Johnson, who occupied a reviewing stand at a location used for the same purpose in Inaugural parades ever since. Here we see General Sherman leading his army and in the act of saluting the President.

Junior League of Washington

Among the President's most difficult decisions were those involving soldiers under death sentences. He prevented executions where he could. On a sentence ordering a Private Scott to be shot for sleeping on post, he asked that "it not take place today." It never did. On the margin of another he wrote, "If you haven't shot Barney D_____ yet, don't!"

For a man so experienced in political matters, he sometimes showed himself ingenuous. Stopping his Secretary of War once he said, "Stanton, how can I get a pension matter straightened up? I've promised an old mother to fix it up for her son, and I've spent all day watching and waiting." "Did you tell them you were the President?" asked Stanton. "No," said Lincoln, "that didn't seem just the thing to do; I ought to have got it as a citizen."

On April 11, 1865 he delivered his last speech to a throng gathered in the rain on the White House lawn. Speaking from the window above the main entrance he began, "We meet this evening not in sorrow but in gladness of heart . . ." Tad, the President's son, scrambled unseen around the floor catching the pages as they fell one by one from his father's hand. Deep in the crowd outside, John Wilkes Booth listened to the President's plan for restoring the South to the Union, for achieving a peace of reconciliation, which included the vote for the Freedmen. Booth turned to his friend Herold and said, "That means nigger citizenship! Now, by God, I'll put him through!"

Secretary Welles went to the White House on the day Lincoln died. Welles saw Tad looking out a window at the foot of the stairs. Tad looked at him, crying, and asked, "Who killed my father?"

52.
The Rathbone House

After passing the White House look to the right up Jackson Place, which borders Lafayette Park on the west side. The third house from Pennsylvania Avenue belonged to Major Henry Rathbone, a name linked to both profound national and personal tragedy.

When General and Mrs. Grant were unable to accompany the Lincolns to Ford's Theater on the evening of April 14, 1865, Mrs. Lincoln hurriedly extended an invitation to Miss Clara Harris, daughter of Senator Ira Harris of New York, and her fiance, Major Rathbone. The major was a close neighbor of the President on Lafayette Square. A White House carriage took the whole party to Ford's Theater, arriving about 8:30 P.M.

Absorbed in the play, Major Rathbone was startled when the pistol shot ripped suddenly through the quietness of the presidential box. Partly stunned, he looked through the drifting smoke and saw a figure, standing behind the President's rocker, drop a pistol to the floor. Mr. Lincoln's head had fallen back against the rocker.

He struggled to his feet and lunged at the man, John Wilkes Booth. Booth struck out at Rathbone with a large knife, wounding him severely in the upper arm. Rathbone again clutched desperately at Booth, but was brushed loose as Booth vaulted over the front railing of the box to the stage ten feet below, narrowly missing a musician. Rathbone, in full view of the audience, his arm drenched with blood, watched Booth limp across the stage and yelled, "Stop that man!" Mrs. Lincoln and Miss Harris stared at him, their faces frozen in shock.

Clara Harris and Major Rathbone later married and in due course moved to Germany. Major Rathbone's mind became deranged and, late in 1885, he tried to kill his children. Thwarted, he then shot his wife to death and stabbed himself. He recovered physically to spend the rest of his life in an insane asylum.

The townhouse at 712 Jackson Place that once belonged to Major Rathbone.
Susan C. Lee

53.
Blair House

The old mansion at 1653 Pennsylvania Avenue stands on the north side of the Avenue, well past the middle of the block next to the old Corcoran Art Gallery (now called Renwick Gallery). Since President Franklin D. Roosevelt's time, Blair House has been joined to the Samuel Phillips Lee mansion next door as the President's guest house for visiting heads of state.

Old Francis P. Blair, a behind-the-scene's power in the Republican Party, and onetime member of President Jackson's "kitchen" cabinet, received Colonel Robert E. Lee of Arlington House in his son's home on April 18, 1861. Acting for President Lincoln, he offered the command of the Union Army to Colonel Lee who had been ordered home from Texas by his friend of Mexican War days, General Winfield Scott, now general-in-chief of the Army. Scott was making a special effort to find experienced leaders for high positions in the U.S. Army at the time of approaching civil war.

Blair House, next to the Renwick Gallery (Old Corcoran Gallery).
Susan C. Lee

Colonel Lee politely rejected the offer. Though opposed to secession, he could take no part in invasion of the southern states. A profoundly troubled man, torn between life-long loyalties to his country and to his state, he travelled south four days later to offer his services to Virginia, which had just seceded from the Union. General Scott said Lincoln had lost a comman-

der worth 50,000 men. In retrospect it appears that Scott may have undervalued General Lee.

The rest is history, and one of the fascinating, deathless legends of our country—how Lee led the Army of Northern Virginia through four years of war and incredible victories to a final exhausted defeat before the larger armies and greater resources of a determined North.

54.
Old Corcoran Art Gallery (Renwick Gallery)

To the right, on the northeast corner of Seventeenth Street and Pennsylvania Avenue, is the red brick old Corcoran Art Gallery in the French Third Empire style. Today known as the Renwick Gallery, after its architect, it contains changing exhibitions of American crafts, decorative arts and design under the auspices of the Smithsonian Institution.

Walking up the formal front steps of banker W. W. Corcoran's brand new art gallery in 1861, a newcomer to town might have been startled to find a sentry at the door and considerable bustle within. The Army had taken it over for the duration.

The first three years of the war saw the Gallery used as the Quartermaster's largest point of issue in the city for uniforms, tents and equippage. It expanded to take over houses and buildings in a two-block sprawling complex of warehouses extending north from the Gallery. This beehive of activity for refitting troops moving to and from the Virginia battlefields issued, at times, as many as a thousand cases of clothing a day.

Quartermaster General Montgomery C. Meigs, whom one could rightly call a man for all seasons, had offices here the last year of the war. He was a noted engineer, a skillful architect, a talented painter of landscapes, a regular army officer and a friend, advisor and expeditor for the President. His authority spread throughout the Union, wherever there were troops to supply and ammunition to move. In Washington alone he employed more than 10,000 people. That the Union soldiers were better fed and cared for than their southern counterparts is due not only to the North's greater resources, but also to Meig's skill and energy.

But by late 1864 Meigs was a grieving, embittered man. His Lieutenant son, John, whom he doted on, was dead, ambushed in western Virginia by guerillas. Meigs had old friends serving the southern side, but he had turned against them. This was not unusual as the war accelerated to its deadly and bitter culmination. He, more than anyone else, was probably responsible for opening Arlington Estate as a cemetery for the soldier dead of both sides, making it impossible for the Lees to return.

Today both Meigs and his son lie side by side behind Arlington House. John's tomb bears a sculpture depicting him as his body was found, lying clad in full uniform with a pistol by his hand.

The old Corcoran Art Gallery in an early postwar photograph. Temporary army buildings just behind the Gallery supported the Gallery's role (1861–1864) as a main Quartermaster Issue Point in the city. The last year of the war the building served as the headquarters of General Meigs, the Union chief of supply and transportation during the war.
National Archives

MAP 11.

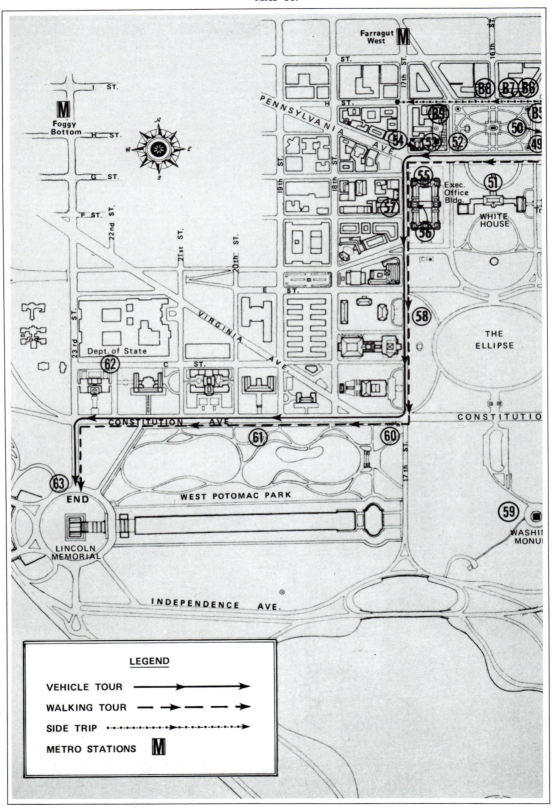

Lower Seventeenth Street and Constitution Avenue. Central City Tour ends.

The Executive Office Building, now used by the White House staff, occupies the site of the Civil War War and Navy Departments. The construction of this huge building for its time (starting in 1871) provided a final signal to the country that the nation's capital would remain at Washington.
Susan C. Lee

LOWER SEVENTEENTH STREET AND CONSTITUTION AVENUE

Vehicle Tour —Turn left (south) into Seventeenth Street, driving seven blocks (counting to your right) to Constitution Avenue. Turn right (west) on Constitution Avenue and drive six blocks west to Twenty-third Street. Turn left on Twenty-third Street and drive one block to the Lincoln Memorial. This ends the central city tour.

Walking Tour —Turn left on Seventeenth Street and walk south somewhat less than a half-mile to Constitution Avenue. Turn right on Constitution Avenue taking the left (south) sidewalk. You will pass close to a new Japanese garden and lake on your left with a good view of marble government buildings to your right. After a half-mile walk through West Potomac Park or by sidewalk you will arrive at the Lincoln Memorial.

Services—Walkers joining the tour on Pennsylvania Avenue or Seventeenth Street should use FARRAGUT WEST METRO STOP. Once at the Lincoln Memorial you are not close to METRO. However, the Park Service's Tourmobile stops here and can return you quickly to the SMITHSONIAN METRO STOP or the Capitol Hill and Union Station areas.

Parking lots thin out fast once you move south from Pennsylvania Avenue on Seventeenth Street. You will be obliged to park along Constitution Avenue or in one of the streets near the Lincoln Memorial. Frequently parking is difficult.

There are few if any eating places on lower Seventeenth Street and Constitution Avenue, but you can buy soft drinks, candy and sandwiches at mobile stands near the Lincoln Memorial front entrance during the tourist season.

55.
The War Department

The original site of the War Department is to the left, on the southeast corner of Seventeenth Street and Pennsylvania Avenue, where the north wing of the Executive Office Building, a large Victorian structure, now stands. The War Department of Civil War days, a modest brick building with a columned entrance way, was the hub of the Union war effort. Only the entrance columns remain, moved to Arlington Cemetery where they serve as ceremonial gateways.

Here were the offices of Lincoln's able, eccentric, forceful workhorse of a Secretary of War, Edwin L. Stanton. Among the faults of this gifted man was a passion for intrigue. Sad to say, there is suspicion that he was not wholly loyal to any of the three Presidents he served as a Cabinet member. A few students even believe he was personally implicated in Lincoln's murder. His lack of humor and his abruptness and arrogance earned him the universal dislike of Washington officialdom. He didn't care. John Grover, manager of the National Theater, once asked Mr. Lincoln why he didn't fire Stanton. Responded Lincoln, "If they'll find me a man who will do his work, I'll dismiss him."

Stanton had none of Lincoln's forbearance. Walking to work one morning he stopped to see General McClellan at his headquarters on Lafayette Square. McClellan kept the Secretary waiting. Stanton told his own chief clerk later, "That will be the last time General McClellan will give either myself or the President the waiting snub!" He was a dangerous, resourceful enemy. A few days later the General went out of town. Stanton immediately moved the Army telegraph equipment and its operators from McClellan's to his own office. By this single step he not only taught the General a bitter lesson, but provided himself with first access to the war news.

Even Mr. Lincoln had to walk through the President's Park day and night on his way to the War Department to keep abreast of the war news. Wrapped in an old-fashioned shawl and seated among the telegraph operators, he would read through the sheaf of recent telegrams. During hours of anxious waiting he found it a quiet place to work and think; he also enjoyed swapping stories with the telegraphers, and occasionally joined them in an oyster supper.

The War Department's front lawn sometimes reflected the growing success of the Union in the later years of the war. After battles that turned out well, captured cannon and other trophies were sometimes brought to Washington and displayed in front of the building. The rows of field artillery and caissons, captured from General Early at the Battle of Cedar Creek, were especially reassuring, for Early had given the city a dreadful scare at Fort Stevens only that past July. When someone discovered that the caissons still held powder loads, they were hurried off to the Arsenal.

There were some odd sights at the War Department in those last jubilant days of the war. Hockerston's Rebel Brigade Band, which had just been captured at Petersburg, were marched to the War Department to serenade Mr. Stanton. The onlookers were delighted. The band played all the southern favorites: "Old Virginia Shore," "Dan Tucker," "Jordan," "Aint we Glad to Get Out of the Wilderness," and of course "Dixie." Asked to please play the National Anthem, they "regretted that they were out of practice."

Edwin L. Stanton, Lincoln's Secretary of War, a brilliant workaholic, profoundly distrusted by his own generation and an enigma to this day. *National Archives*

The War Department of the Civil War. Its nerve center was War Secretary Stanton's office and its telegraph office. *National Archives*

56.
The Navy Department

About a block south down Seventeenth on the left (east) about opposite its intersection with F Street, is the site of the small brick Navy Department of Civil War days. The space is now occupied by the center block of the Executive Office Building.

Navy Secretary Gideon Welles was the irascible, industrious leader of the naval side of the war. He was once described as looking like an exasperated Santa Claus, because of a flowing white beard and abundant white wig to match. A newspaper man from Hartford, Connecticut, Mr. Welles knew nothing about ships when he arrived. But he was solid, capable and more balanced by far than Stanton. He grew with the task of expanding the Navy from a few modern steamers to probably the best striking and blockading naval force of the age.

Mr. Welles was loyal to Mr. Lincoln and, through his diary, left a fascinating story of the inner workings of the Lincoln Cabinet. This shrewd Yankee was hard to fool. Commenting in his dairy about news after a battle, he wrote, "When I get nothing clear . . . I have my apprehensions . . . Adverse tidings are suppressed with a deal of fuss and mystery, a shuffling over of papers and maps, and a far-reaching vacant gaze"

He was unruffled under pressure. On March 9, 1862, Mr. Lincoln and his top war leaders gathered at the White House in great distress. *Merrimac*, a "new-fangled" southern ironclad warship, was reported to be sinking the Union wood-hulled warships one after the other in Hampton Roads. There was apparently no way to stop her, and Mr. Stanton feared *Merrimac* might steam up the Potomac. At any moment the ironclad could come into view and lob shells into a helpless Washington. Even the President was infected by Mr. Stanton's fears and looked anxiously down the Potomac from the window.

Excellent view of mid-nineteenth century Washington (about 1870) showing Seventeenth Street with the War and Navy Departments clearly visible. The Winder Building, Union Army headquarters, is in the center foreground. *Library of Congress →*

115

Welles quietly told them there was hope. A new Federal ironclad called *Monitor* had arrived in Hampton Roads to engage *Merrimac.* He reassured them that the Potomac was too shallow for the deep draft of *Merrimac* to come up river; she could not threaten Washington. The next day Mr. Welles' views were vindicated. The two ironclads, in a historic battle that forever changed naval warfare, fought to a draw. People were amazed when they saw this curious ship a few weeks later at the Navy Yard for repairs. The whole country called it a cheesebox on a raft.

Mr. Welles cared deeply for the President, and his diary reflects this feeling in a reserved New England way. During the whole of the night of Mr. Lincoln's death watch, he stayed at the Petersen House. He went on to serve President Johnson with the same fealty and ability.

57.
Union Army Headquarters (The Winder Building)

Now restored to its 1865 exterior appearance, this building stands to the right on the northwest corner of Seventeenth and F Streets. Built by General Winder (the man who lost the nearby Battle of Bladensburg to the British in 1814) it was the first of scores of buildings built cheaply and on speculation for lease to the government. It had other firsts. The Winder Building pioneered in the use of steel beams in construction, and in the use of central heating in Washington. Its five floors qualified it as a highrise in those days.

At 532 Seventeenth Street, across F Street from the Winder Building and on the southwest corner, stood a modest residential building. After Lee's defeat (April 9, 1865) General Grant moved his headquarters back to Washington and set up offices here. During the 1940's the house was demolished.

Martin Luther King Library

The Honorable Gideon Welles, Secretary of the Navy in both the Lincoln and Johnson cabinets.

National Archives

Popular Matthew Brady photograph of Mr. Lincoln and his son Tad. The President was concerned that viewers of this photo might assume that Tad and he were looking at the Bible, not the case.
National Archives

During the war the building was used as Union Army Headquarters, a sort of forerunner to the present day Pentagon. A succession of high Union commanders had offices here, among them General Winfield Scott (Old Fuss and Feathers), General George McClellan (Little Mac), General Henry W. Halleck (Old Brains), and General Ulysses S. Grant (Unconditional Surrender). Then as now the troops gave the brass names.

General Grant spent as little time as possible in his office here, heeding the advice of his friend, General Sherman, who urged him to stay away from the political and personal infighting that engulfed a general in Washington. Running the Army from his headquarters with the Army in Virginia, Grant returned to Washington only rarely. On one of his brief visits, he was almost caught by some southern partisans raiding along the Orange and Alexandria rail line.

The fifth floor of the Winder Building was used as a hospital briefly in 1862, and it was rumored that some Confederate prisoners were kept there to work around the place. The rest of the space was used by some of the Army bureau chiefs and their staffs (Ordnance, Engineer and Military Justice, etc.). On the roof was an Army signal station where signal flags continually wigwagged, "talking" to the forts and outlying posts by relay as far away as Fairfax Court House and south of Alexandria. On April 10, 1865, the signallers got a sudden holiday and the roof activity was stilled. General Lee had surrendered.

As was his habit, the President rarely waited in his office for people to come to him. He came often to the Winder Building, and Noah Brooks worried about his safety, walking alone through the President's Park at night. He knew about the threatening mail the President was receiving.

58.
The White Lot (The Ellipse)

To the left of Seventeenth Street, after you pass E Street, notice the park south of the White House, with its tall trees. Now known as the Ellipse, it was then called the White Lot for no better reason than that there was a white-painted wooden fence around it. The Ellipse was larger in those days. Sometime after the Civil War the portion north of E Street was absorbed into the White House grounds and closed to the public.

Lincoln's newspaperman friend, Noah Brooks, tells that one day Tad, the President's small son, pointed out to his father that Jack, his pet turkey, had wandered out among the soldiers of a Pennsylvania regiment camped on the White Lot. (Jack had earlier escaped becoming Thanksgiving dinner at Tad's intercession.) The Presidential election of 1864 was at hand, and polls had been set up in the camp at which the soldiers were voting. Watching Jack peck about among the soldiers, Mr. Lincoln asked Tad what business the turkey had in stalking about the polls. "Does he vote?" he inquired. "No," said Tad, "He is not of age."

Two small temporary camps were built on the White Lot—Rush and Reynolds Barracks. They were used when need arose as hospitals, barracks for soldiers on duty in the city, or as bivouacs for troops passing through. Pennsylvania regiments on their way to and from Virginia customarily camped there.

59.
The Washington Monument (The Beef Depot Monument)

As you turn right from Seventeenth Street into Constitution, the Washington Monument is on the left, in the middle of the Mall.

By the time of the Civil War, the Washington Monument had fallen on sad days. It was begun in pomp and

The Winder Building, Headquarters of the Union Army, is restored to its exterior Civil War appearance.
Susan C. Lee

The Monument Grounds just south of the junction of Fifteenth Street and Constitution Avenue (then the City Canal) was used as an army slaughter house and grazing area for cattle. This and other parts of the Mall were also used as troop bivouac areas, and as a place to test army weapons, explosives and other new equipment.

Library of Congress

high hopes with the cornerstone-laying on July 4, 1848, but chronic shortages of funds and curious misadventures in management had weakened public support. By 1861 the project had been more or less abandoned. Around the truncated column, only 156 feet high, were a few ramshackle sheds for storing stone-block gifts, intended for the interior walls.

Nearby, on the Mall just south of the canal at the bottom of Fifteenth Street, the wartime business of the grounds began.

In May of 1861 a large herd of cattle was brought across the canal to pasture here, awaiting slaughter to feed the incoming soldiers. Some of the herd fell in the canal and drowned. Undaunted, the Army brought more cattle in and built a slaughterhouse. It was a group of pens and sheds soon "surrounded by offal rotting two or three feet deep." This nuisance to the city continued for the balance of the war. Walt Whitman remembers seeing 10,000 beeves on the hoof grazing near here.

The war saw other uses for the Monument grounds.

Space was at such a premium in the city that transient troops sometimes billeted nearby. Both mounted and infantry troops conducted training near the neglected, abbreviated shaft, a fitting symbol of the state of the Union at that time. Occasionally, new weapons and other experimental military hardware were tested here. The President sometimes attended, fascinated by the new technology. At least once he took part personally, firing one of the new repeating rifles at a group of targets.

60.
Washington's Canals

You are approaching the intersection of Seventeenth Street and Constitution Avenue, one of Washington's most interesting corners.

In this print of galloping horsemen, war artist Thomas Nast shows a Federal artillery battery training on the Washington Monument Grounds.

Junior League of Washington

Constitution Avenue today runs in the trace of two old canals. One, the Chesapeake & Ohio Canal, started in Cumberland, Maryland, descended southeast along the north shores of the Potomac through Georgetown, thence to this location. Here it met the old City Canal at a point where both canals opened into the Potomac River.

On October 24, 1861 Union casualties from the disaster at Ball's Bluff near Leesburg were brought forty miles by canal boat down the Chesapeake & Ohio Canal to hospitals in the city. They were mercifully spared the agonizing journey over rutted roads in jolting wagons, the ordeal of most men suffering from battle wounds in the Civil War. However, the journey must have been a slow and frustrating one for the men confined to the holds and cabins of dirty canal boats usually carrying cargoes of coal and lumber.

The City Canal ran eastward from this point along what is now Constitution Avenue to a turning basin behind the Center Market, the present site of the National Archives Building. Continuing farther east, the Canal proceeded to the base of Capitol Hill, then jogged southeast to terminate at the Anacostia River near the Navy Yard.

The two canals fell victim to the Baltimore & Ohio Railroad's ability to haul tonnages into the city faster and cheaper. The City Canal, long an eyesore and a hazard to health, was the first to go. The city must have heaved a collective sigh of relief when it was filled during the 1870's. The Chesapeake & Ohio Canal from

From this balloonist's view of the city in 1861, the City Canal with its iron bridges and entrance into the Potomac River is clearly visible.

National Archives

View of the Chesapeake and Ohio Canal not far from Harper's Ferry in early July, 1864. Near here General Early's 12,000 men crossed the Potomac River enroute to attack Washington. Notice the nearby Potomac to the right, the upended canal boat and the ongoing sabotage of the canal banks.

Martin Luther King Library

Cumberland to Georgetown hung on much longer, until the 1920's. The National Park Service has restored portions of it, and the route today is a scenic National park, ideal for hikers and boaters.

On the southwest corner of this intersection is the last surviving relic of both canals in the downtown city —the old, stone lock keeper's house.

61.
The North Potomac Shores

Leaving Seventeenth Street, head west on Constitution Avenue.

A canal boater of Civil War days, relaxing on his cabin roof and gliding slowly west by mule-power on the Chesapeake & Ohio Canal, could not have believed his eyes if he had glimpsed what you now see to the left of Constitution Avenue.

Instead of trees and green parkland, with the Lincoln Memorial for a centerpiece, he would have seen beyond the tow path and a thin fringe of bushes only the broad, muddy expanses of the Potomac River, broken here and there by mud shoals.

The land to the left of Constitution Avenue is all manmade, the work of the Army Corps of Engineers from 1874 to 1913. The filling of this large area was necessary to overcome the severe, periodic flooding of the lower city and to eradicate the other health hazards of the Potomac flats. These malaria-producing mud-banks and swamps held stagnant waters all along the city's northern Potomac shoreline. This project also produced a bonus—one of the city's chief charms—East and West Potomac Parks.

62.
The City's Cruelest Fire

Moving west on Constitution Avenue, look right on Twenty-second street to where the white walls of the State Department now rise.

The area of the present State Department Building, and much more besides, was Camp Fuller (1861–1863), an immense Army Remount Depot where some say as many as 30,000 horses and mules were stabled. A fire of unknown origin suddenly burst out between six and seven o'clock the cold, dark night of December 26, 1861. The flames spread rapidly through the low, pine stables, each several hundred feet long, which housed the animals. Some two hundred horses were immediately smothered or "literally burnt at the stake," as the *Evening Star* reported. The scene was "awful to the extreme."

At great peril to themselves, a few soldiers and civilians entered the holocaust with knives and axes, and cut the halters of all the horses they could reach. Over 1,000 horses, mad with fear, galloped into every quarter of the city. The next day droves of them were rounded up and returned to the corrals. Some were found in Georgetown, others as they wandered around Rock Creek Park; a large herd had galloped wildly down Massachusetts Avenue and were scattered as far east as the Capitol. Some had even crossed the bridges of the City Canal and were found grazing on the Mall.

At least 150 horses lay injured about the city. Some had broken their legs; some lay scorched and blackened in the streets. A number were in such pain they could not be approached and had to be shot. One horse somehow found its way into the south enclosure of the Treasury where, burned and exhausted, it died.

Although the cause of the fire was unknown, scarcely a week passed before an "incendiary" had made an attempt to complete the incineration of the stables. Perhaps because of the hazards presented so close to the city, and the unruly presence of great numbers of teamsters, the stables were moved in mid-1863 across the Anacostia River to Geisboro Point. Here, in this more remote and spacious site, the remount activities of the Army of the Potomac continued for the remainder of the war.

Contemporary version of the great fire at the Government Stables at the present location of the State Department, December 26, 1861.
Junior League of Washington

Just before you turn left from Constitution Avenue to approach the Lincoln Memorial on Twenty-third Street, notice the hill rising to your right (northwest). On its crest sat in Civil War times the scientific pride of the nation, the Washington Observatory. Here Matthew Fountain Maury made his notable discoveries of the influence of tides and winds on sea navigation. Like many others, he went south at the beginning of the war.

Notice the black ball suspended from the pole on top of the dome. At precisely noon every day, celestial time, it slid down the pole; fascinated Washingtonians set their watches and marveled at the wonders of science.

Library of Congress

63.
The Lincoln Memorial

As we look at this classic marble temple, dedicated to Mr. Lincoln, the impression is one of serenity and peace.

No more for him life's stormy conflicts
Nor victory, nor defeat—no more time's dark events,
Charging like ceaseless clouds across the sky.

from "Hush'd the Camps Today" by Walt Whitman

On entering the Memorial one stares up at the majestic seated figure of the President wondering, "What was he really like?" As the great political leader of the Union he was, and had to be, many things to many people. At the same time, he seems to have kept his own counsel, preferring not to disclose his inner thoughts and purposes readily. This may be why he puzzled people so much, and why so many stories grew up about him, each illustrating some aspect of the Lincoln personality. These passages give us no more than brief glimpses of the man.

Lincoln on himself—"It may be said I am in height six feet four inches, nearly; lean in flesh, weighing on an average one hundred and eighty pounds; dark complexion, with coarse black hair and gray eyes."

Carl Sandburg, *Abraham Lincoln the War Years*

Lincoln in conversation—"And when he spoke a miracle occurred. The dull, listless features dropped like a mask. The eyes began to sparkle, the mouth to smile, the whole countenance was wreathed in animation so that a stranger would have said, 'Why, this man, so angular and somber a moment ago, is really handsome.'"

Horace White, *Chicago Tribune*

Lincoln at ease—When "the time came to laugh, he would sometimes throw his left foot across his right knee, clenching his foot with both hands and bending forward, his whole frame seemed to be convulsed . . ."

Congressman George W. Julian

The good man—I went to the White House today and saw the President. He is a very tall man. He is not a handsome man. He is not graceful. But he is good . . . Commonly he is sober, but sometimes he laughs, and when he laughs, he laughs very much and opens his mouth very deep . . ."

Frederick Law Olmstead to his 12-year-old son

The tired man—"He was in his plain two-horse barouche, and looked very much worn and tired; the lines, indeed, of vast responsibilities, intricate questions and demands of life and death cut deeper than ever upon his dark brown face."

Walt Whitman

The friend of the blacks—"I was impressed with his entire freedom from popular prejudice against the colored race. He was the first great man that I talked with in the United States freely, who in no single instance reminded me of the difference between himself and myself . . ."

Frederick Douglass

The war leader—"General Sheridan says, 'If the thing (the battle) is pressed I think that Lee will surrender.' Let the thing be pressed."

Message from Mr. Lincoln to General Grant

The peace maker—"He wanted peace on almost any terms, and there is no knowing what proposals he might have been willing to listen to. His heart was tenderness throughout, and, as long as the rebels laid down their arms, he did not care how it was done."

Admiral Porter, recollections

The Lincoln funeral parade winds down Fifteenth Street into Pennsylvania Avenue, making its way from the White House to the Capitol.

Junior League of Washington

Photograph of Mr. Lincoln taken by Alexander Gardner April 10, 1865, four days before his death. It shows a slightly smiling but very worn president. The war was ending and he was very happy in these final days of his life. *National Archives*

PART III

Side
Trips

Tour B.

MAP 12.

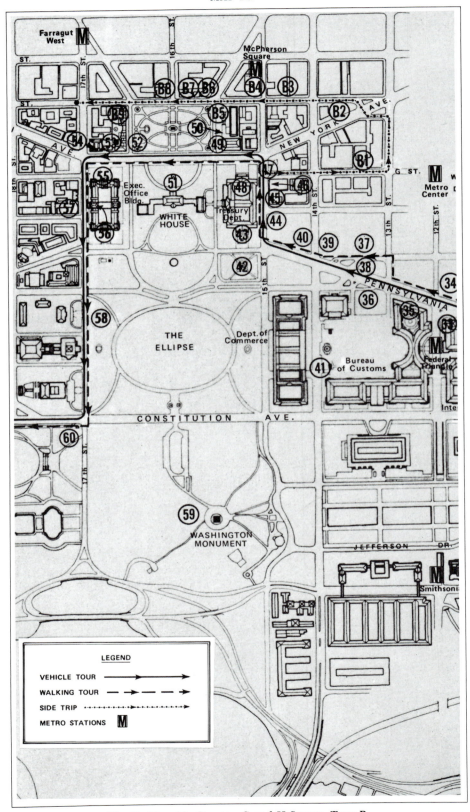

The Fashionable Quarter, G and H Streets. Tour B.

A view of the White House grounds south of the mansion in August, 1861. Prince Napoleon of France is visiting the Lincolns, and the dignitaries are on the balcony before dinner listening to a band concert.

National Archives

THE FASHIONABLE QUARTER OF CIVIL WAR WASHINGTON
G AND H STREETS NW—TOUR B

Vehicle Tour—Turn right from Fifteenth Street onto G Street, proceeding east for two blocks, turn left on Thirteenth Street for one block. Then turn left on New York Avenue and follow the lane leading right (northwest) into H Street. You pass directly in front of the New York Avenue Presbyterian Church.

Walking Tour—Follow the same route as the Vehicle Tour above. Walkers taking METRO to enter or leave this district can use MCPHERSON SQUARE, METRO CENTER or FARRAGUT WEST STOPS, whichever is closer.

Services—There are commercial parking lots on G and Thirteenth Streets. Once you reach H Street there is little commercial parking available and street parking is hard to find. However, commercial lots are one block away along I Street.

There are places for lunch along the route. The closer you come to the junction of H and Seventeenth Streets the better selection of eating places you have.

B-1.
They Placed the Wounded on Highbacked Pews— Epiphany Church

Proceed east on G Street from Fifteenth. Halfway between Fourteenth and Thirteenth Streets, on the left, is the graceful white structure of Epiphany Church, long an oasis of serenity in this commercial district.

The loyalties of the congregation of Epiphany Church were deeply split between North and South. On a Sunday in March of 1862 the Episcopalian bishop had requested a prayer read that he had written "for the deliverance of the District from the terrors of blockade and siege." The Confederates had just abandoned gun positions along the Virginia shore that had made boat travel on the Potomac hazardous. Sunday services in the city's Episcopal churches were a catastrophe. Three ministers refused to read the prayer at all; where it *was* read, there were red, angry faces and sudden departures from the churches, followed by unseemly exchanges outside. Afterwards, Dr. Hall of Epiphany pled with the bishop "not to compose such prayers in the future without consulting all the ministers'' first. Discord was present in other denominations too. An abolitionist minister preached a sermon at his Presbyterian church on 4½ Street that nearly destroyed his parish.

On July 2, 1862, a long line of horsedrawn ambulances pulled to a halt on G Street outside of Epiphany Church. Bystanders watched as wounded men were carried inside on stretchers and laid on the cushions of the highbacked pews. For the injured this was paradise compared to the jolting bed of a railroad flatcar or the crowded deck of a river steamer. The congregation forgot its differences to help in the emergency. A number became nurses, including the seven McKean sisters who served as volunteers for the remainder of the war.

The congregation of another Episcopal church, Trinity, was startled during one Sunday service in June 1862 to hear the loud crash of lumber falling on the sidewalk outside. The Army had decided to convert the church into a hospital that same day. The customary procedure was simply to build a wood floor over the pews and place cots on the new flooring. By early 1863 the Army was far enough along in the construction of its new, large pavilion-style hospitals to begin returning these churches to their parishes.

B-2.
The New York Avenue Presbyterian Church

Turn left on Thirteenth Street and drive north one block to New York Avenue. The church is on the corner of New York Avenue and H Street. As you approach it, take a left turn into the H Street lane. Be careful; this is a complicated turn to make.

In early 1861, President and Mrs. Lincoln decided to attend the New York Avenue Presbyterian Church and did so regularly throughout the war. A Lincoln family pew has been retained in the present church in about the same location it held in the earlier church. Whenever a president of the United States is present for services, he is seated in the Lincoln pew.

In July 1862 the Army was in dire need of more hospital space. Dr. Gurley, pastor of New York Avenue

Epiphany Church on G Street between Fourteenth and Thirteenth Streets—for a time in 1862 a Union military hospital. *Susan C. Lee*

The New York Avenue Presbyterian Church. The church where the Lincoln family worshiped during the Civil War was torn down and replaced on the same site by a modern one some years ago. But the old Lincoln pew remains in the new church, and outside on New York Avenue can be found the hitching post where the Lincoln carriage was tied during services. *Susan C. Lee*

Presbyterian, announced at a Sunday morning service that "religious services would be suspended until further notice as the church was needed as a hospital." The lumber to be used as flooring on top of the pews was stacked in the street outside. On hearing this, President Lincoln stood up in his pew, interrupting, "Dr. Gurley, this action was taken without my consent, and I hereby countermand the order. The churches are needed as never before for divine services."

It seems odd for Mr. Lincoln to have stood up in church as he did on this occasion, but the congregation was used to it. Lincoln held powerful convictions about prayer. He thought a man should stand up at his prayers, and he did so, even though the custom observed in this church was for the congregation to remain seated when praying.

B-3.
H Street

On leaving New York Avenue Presbyterian Church, follow H Street to the west.

This street was the finest address in the wartime city. In its townhouses and mansions, some still surviving, the elite of the city lived—cabinet ministers, generals, senators, wealthy businessmen and the socially prominent.

The fading elegance of H Street calls to mind a stirring moment for George B. McClellan, onetime com-

Where the wealthy of the city lived. Here is the impressive sight that once was H Street during the latter half of the 19th Century, a line of fine mansions one block north of the White House.

Martin Luther King Library

Wartime photograph of General McClellan, for a time the idol of his soldiers.   *National Archives*

mander of the Army of the Potomac. His home was on H Street. To do him special honor, an estimated 20,000 bluecoats marched past his home on September 6, 1862. Their bands blared and the ranks of troops in dusty blue uniforms stretched from sidewalk to sidewalk; the cheering, tumult and dust that late summer day was immense. At a time when the Union cause had never seemed more hopeless it is something of a curiosity that the Army chose to honor McClellan when they could just as easily have marched past the White House —a block away. The men, though none realized it, were bound for a mighty destiny at a small creek in western Maryland called Antietam. There, at heavy cost, they won the first great Union victory in the east.

On the following day, September 7, 1862, Navy Secretary Welles, out for a stroll with his son, saw a party of twenty to thirty horsemen near the junction of Fifteenth and H Streets. They looked closely because of the fine horses in the cavalcade. It was General McClellan and his staff. The General rode over to shake hands, stating that he was on his way north to lead the Army against Lee. "Success to you then, General, go with all

my heart," said the deeply moved Welles. Within two weeks McClellan had his victory, but he let the cornered southern Army get away. Two months later a disgruntled Lincoln, convinced McClellan was stricken with a terminal case of "the slows," fired him for good.

B-4.
General McClellan's House

General McClellan's home, 334 H Street, once stood near the northwest corner of Fifteenth and H Streets, to the right.

On the bright, cool morning of September 2, 1862, swept clear and fresh by yesterday's thunderstorm, General George B. McClellan breakfasted early. He had much to brood about. His Army had been thoroughly beaten by Lee's smaller Army on the Virginia Peninsula, and he had lost his position of command. He realized the Cabinet, especially Treasury Secretary Chase

The Dolley Madison House, onetime Headquarters of the Army of the Potomac.

Susan C. Lee

Drawing of the celebration in front of General George McClellan's home (near the northwest corner of Fifteenth and H Streets) on the evening (November, 1861) of his appointment as general-in-chief of the army. Large numbers of his troops serenaded him to the accompaniment of fireworks.

Library of Congress

and War Secretary Stanton, were close to regarding him as a traitor. Now his beloved Army of the Potomac, led into battle by General John Pope, had taken a fearful beating near the old battlefield of Bull Run.

There was an unexpected knocking at the door. To McClellan's surprise the President and General Henry Halleck were ushered into the room. Obviously both anxious and distressed, Mr. Lincoln bluntly asked the startled McClellan to take command of the city's defenses and Pope's Army as it retreated toward Washington.

Lincoln had to swallow his pride in taking back the difficult, touchy McClellan. But there was no one else the Army trusted; it was McClellan or chaos. The President must have dreaded giving the news to the Cabinet that afternoon. They were aghast.

B-5.
Headquarters of the Army of the Potomac

To your left, on the southeast corner of H Street and Madison Place, is the old house General McClellan used as a headquarters of the Army of the Potomac from November 1861 through March 1862. It was the old Cutts home, where President Madison's widow, Dolley, had lived for many years until her death in 1849. Her charm and friendliness had made the place a center of social life in the capital; people customarily called here after leaving White House receptions.

General McClellan brought skills the Army badly needed in August, 1861. Great organizing abilities were his specialty; he kept the staffs of two other headquarters beside this one hard at work. His general-in-chief's office was in the Winder Building and his Adjutant General's office was on the northwest corner of Seventeenth and Pennsylvania Avenue. The General's style was to spend as little time as possible in these offices. He could often be seen with his staff galloping through the city, on his way to visit forts, camps and depots.

At thirty-six a splendid, commanding figure on horseback, the young general became the idol of his men who were badly in need of someone to look up to after the disaster of Bull Run. Over the months of training that winter, he gave them something vital—discipline, organization and pride—qualities that would carry through many terrible adversities. He also gave them a proud title, The Army of the Potomac.

The genuine misfortune of this gifted man is that the enthusiasm for him in the Army's ranks was not shared by the Administration's leaders. It was his own fault. He seemed to go out of his way to alienate them, one by one, with his display of incredible touchiness and arrogance.

One cool November evening in 1861, Mr. Lincoln, Mr. Seward and John Hay, the President's secretary, strolled across Lafayette Park to visit McClellan. Informed that the General was out, they sat down to wait. After about an hour General McClellan returned and went directly upstairs. Thinking there must be some mistake, the President asked if the General knew they were there. He had been told, came the reply, but he had gone to bed. Mr. Lincoln quietly departed.

Wartime lithograph of the Soldier's Home. The Lincoln Summer White House is the residence just beyond the flag pole. Still there, it is used as a temporary residence for people visiting the aged servicemen.
(Notice the tower to the right. It served as a Union signal station during General Early's 1864 attack on Washington. Its constantly waving signal flags by day and signal lights at night were so active that Rebel General Early later complained that the signalers saw every move his forces made.)

Library of Congress

B-6.
Vermont Avenue, Lincoln's Route to the Soldier's Home

To the right, across the street from Dolley Madison's house, Vermont Avenue angles into Lafayette Square from the northeast. This is the road President Lincoln took often, to and from his summer cottage at the Soldier's Home. Walt Whitman used to watch him pass.

August 12, 1863—"I see the President almost every day. He never sleeps at the White House during the hot season . . . but has quarters at a healthy location some three miles north of the city, the Soldier's Home . . .

"I saw him this morning about 8½ coming in to business, riding on Vermont Avenue . . . He always has a company of twenty-four to thirty cavalry, with sabres drawn and held upright over their shoulders. They say this guard was against his personal wish, but he let his counselors have their way . . .

"Mr. Lincoln on the saddle generally rides a good-sized easy going gray horse, is dress'd in plain black, somewhat rusty and dusty, wears a black stiff hat, and looks about as ordinary in attire, etc., as the commonest man. A lieutenant, with yellow straps rides at his left, and following behind, two-by-two, comes the cavalrymen, in their yellow-striped jackets. They are generally going at a slow trot, as that is the pace set them by the one they wait upon. The sabres and accoutrements clank, and the entirely unornamental cortege, as it trots toward Lafayette Square arouses no sensation . . ."

B-7.
St. John's Church

The old white painted church is to the right on the northeast corner of Sixteenth and H Streets.

St. John's Church, its appearance unchanged since the war, is one of the most historic buildings of the city. *Susan C. Lee*

Its church bell is made from British cannon captured in the War of 1812. Its architect, Benjamin Latrobe, was one of the Capital's famous builders, and a gifted amateur musician as well. He was the church's first organist and even wrote the hymn for its dedication in 1816. It was in Civil War days and remains today, one of Washington's most important churches.

On February 25, 1861, his first Sunday in Washington, President-elect Lincoln and his future Secretary of State, William H. Seward, walked up Fifteenth Street from Willard's Hotel, crossed Lafayette Park, and entered St. John's Church. They were seated in Mr. Seward's pew for the service.

Constance Green, in her history of the Church, tells of one Sunday morning service at St. John's. Mrs. John Rogers sat nervously in her pew on March 9, 1862, concerned about the shocking news just arrived that Sunday morning. The Confederate ironclad, *Merrimac*, had steamed out of Norfolk harbor and was sinking the Union's wooden warships at Hampton Roads.

"The church bell brought the people in at the last minute. In the middle of Mr. Pyne's sermon the sexton came down the aisle, touched Mr. Fox, the Assistant Secretary of the Navy, and whispered something. Mr. Fox hastily went out. Then the sexton came down the other aisle of the church and bent over the general in command of the defense of Washington and he departed at once. The sexton came again and took out old Commodore Smith whose son was captain of the *Con*-gress. When he was told that the *Congress* had surrendered, he said, 'The *Congress* surrendered!—then my Joe is dead!' Then General Meigs went out, and then Mr. Pyne clapped his sermon book together and gave the benediction, and the congregation came out in fear and trembling, wondering when they would see the *Merrimack* coming up the Potomac River to bombard the White House and the rest of Washington . . .''

B-8.
Mrs. Greenhow's House, or "Fort Greenhow"

In the fall of 1861 the press awarded the nickname "Fort Greenhow" to a small house on the west side of Sixteenth Street across from St. John's Church, about the present location of the Hay-Adams Hotel.

It was the home of the glamorous, socially prominent widow, Mrs. Rose O'Neal Greenhow, one of the most famous spies of the Civil War. Tourists would pause outside the house, ogle at the marching guard, and hope to catch a glimpse of her. The whole North believed that she had used her irresistible charms on im-

Like two prehistoric monsters, the Monitor and Merrimac fight to a draw at Hampton Roads, Virginia, March 9, 1862.

National Archives

portant northern leaders to obtain military information. After transcribing the information into a secret cypher, people said, she sent it through the lines to General Beauregard, commander of the Confederate forces at Bull Run. After the war these rumors were borne out. It was discovered that her message of July 15, 1861, reporting the Union Army's advance on Centreville, reached the Confederates in time to bring not one but two armies to bear against the hapless Federals at the First Battle of Bull Run.

On August 23, 1861 Mrs. Greenhow had just returned to her front door from her daily promenade. Two men stepped forward to arrest her, one of them Allan Pinkerton, chief of the Army's Secret Service. Taking her inside quietly, the detectives waited, hoping to snare some of her accomplices. However little Rose, Mrs. Greenhow's daughter, slipped outside, climbed a tree and shouted out to one and all, "Mother's been arrested!"

In spite of the closest surveillance, Mrs. Greenhow always succeeded in destroying incriminating papers and still remained in contact with the Confederate government. Her home was turned into a female prison, and other ladies of doubtful loyalty were brought there. By January 1862 the Army was out of patience. They closed "Fort Greenhow" sending the dangerous, resourceful lady to the Old Capitol Prison. By chance, her cell was the very room in which she had cared for her husband's friend, Senator John C. Calhoun, in his final days.

Some months later Mrs. Greenhow and little Rose were sent through the lines to Richmond where still further adventures began. She eventually drowned in 1864 while trying to return to the Confederacy from England. Fearing that Federal blockading ships would capture her, she transferred to a small boat off Fort Fisher, North Carolina. It swamped in the turbulent water, and she was swept beneath the surface by a bag of gold coins tied around her waist.

Mrs. Greenhow's house under guard in the fall of 1861. It became for several months a prison for women charged with disloyal activities against the United States. *Martin Luther King Library*

B-9.
Decatur House

This beautifully preserved early nineteenth century mansion in the Federal style owned by the National Trust for Historic Preservation is on the southwest corner of Jackson Place and H Street.

After the White House, Decatur House was the second home built on Lafayette Square; the great Naval hero of the War of 1812, Stephen Decatur, lived there briefly before being killed in a duel. During the Civil War the Army used it as the headquarters of the Commissary General of the Union Army and for storage. Its interest to us is in the years preceding the war.

In 1842 the wealthy Mr. Gadsby bought the old place from Mrs. Decatur. He gave lavish parties here, and the French Minister, Chevalier Adolphe de Barcourt, tells of one of them:

"Some days ago I went to an evening party at Mr. Gadsby's, proprietor of the hotel where I stayed on my arrival here. He is an old wretch who has made a fortune in the slave trade, which does not prevent Washington society from rushing to his house and I should make my government very unpopular if I refused to associate with this kind of people. This gentleman's house is the most beautiful in the city, very well furnished, and perfect in the distribution of the rooms, but the society my God!"

What the Chevalier does not mention is that slaves were kept in the attic and in the long brick ell that fronts

The celebrated Confederate spy, Mrs. Greenhow, with her daughter, Rose. Brady took this photograph when they were imprisoned at the Old Capitol Prison early in 1862.

Library of Congress

on H Street. At night sometimes one could hear their howls and cries. Slave auctions were held from time to time in the mansion's courtyard.

The last resident of Decatur House before the war was Judah P. Benjamin, Senator from Louisiana. When war broke out he went to Richmond to serve as a most competent member of Jefferson Davis' cabinet. Among his posts were Attorney General, Secretary of War and Secretary of State. After the final collapse of the South in 1865, he escaped overseas to become a distinguished British citizen.

Decatur House in the latter years of the 19th Century. Notice the Victorian treatment given the ground floor doors and windows of this Federal-style building. It is now owned by the National Trust for Historic Preservation and is restored to its original appearance.

Martin Luther King Library

PART IV

Sites
of
Interest
in
or near
the
City

Tour C.

MAP 13.

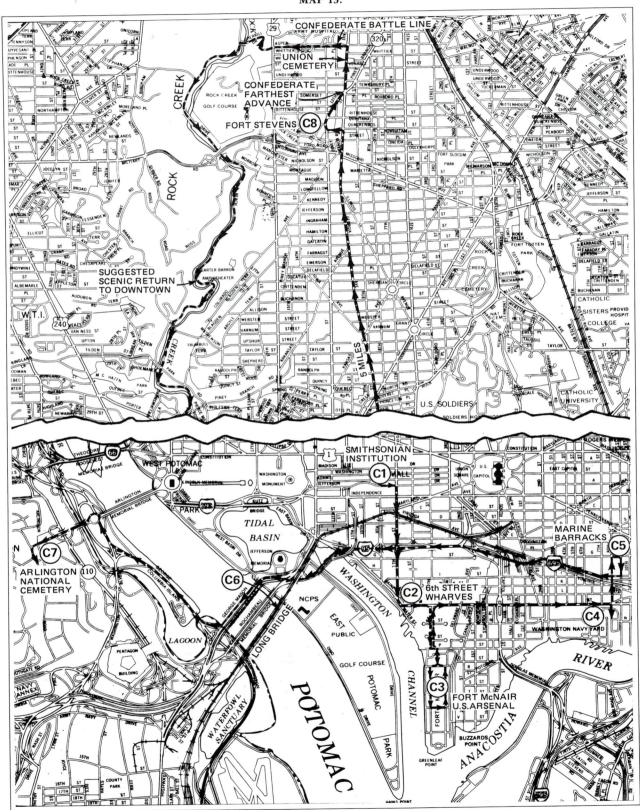

Sites of Interest In or Near the City. Tour C.

Burning of the Smithsonian "Castle" on January 24, 1865. Apparently the artist, Philip Wharton sought a greater dramatic effect for the readers of *Harper's Weekly* by parading a cavalry unit on the front grounds of the burning building. *Library of Congress*

SITES OF INTEREST IN OR NEAR THE CITY—TOUR C

The only convenient way to visit these sights (except the Smithsonian Institution) is by car, using the maps (opposite) and following the directions in the first paragraph of the pages for each location.

All but one of the sights can be grouped for a single trip by vehicle in this order: The Smithsonian "Castle" and Arts and Industries Building, The Sixth Street Wharves, The Washington Arsenal (today's Fort McNair), The Navy Yard, The Marine Barracks, The Long Bridge, and Arlington House (the Lee Mansion).

Arlington House, because of its beauty and historic interest, is recommended for a separate visit. The Navy Yard also, with its Navy and Marine museums and unique atmosphere, deserves a separate trip by those with sea-faring, U.S. Naval or historic interests.

Fort Stevens is recommended for Civil War buffs only because of its distance from the center of town and the approach through a less than scenic part of the city. However, those who do choose to see it can also stop briefly at a tiny National Cemetery one-half mile north of Fort Stevens on the right (east) side of Georgia Avenue. Here, visited by few, are buried some of the Union soldiers of the Sixth Corps killed in the battle in front of Fort Stevens. About two miles farther north on Georgia Avenue to the right in the yard of Grace Church are a monument and graves of a number of Confederate soldiers killed in the same battle. After leaving the Fort Stevens area, a drive of several miles back to the center of the city through nearby Rock Creek Park is suggested. It is perhaps the most pleasant park drive in the District. But avoid the rush hours. The Park Drive is one-way south until 9:30 A.M. and one-way north starting at 3:45 P.M.

C-1.
The Smithsonian Institution

From Pennsylvania Avenue take Seventh Street south across the Mall and park on the left in the parking garage beneath the National Air and Space Museum at Seventh and Independence Avenue. Then walk west on Jefferson Drive about 300 yards to the old Smithsonian castle, a Gothic Revival building finished in 1849.

The castle is the earliest building of this unique institution which operates a number of government museums and art galleries grouped mainly about the Mall. The Smithsonian began with a $500,000 bequest from an Englishman, James Smithson, who never visited this country. He died in Genoa in 1829, leaving the sum for "an establishment for the increase and diffusion of knowledge among men."

The Smithsonian under learned Professor Joseph Henry, a physicist of international repute, had become a center of culture in Washington. Its lecture hall was

Wartime drawing of the Navy Yard from the Anacostia River. Riding at anchor are war vessels awaiting repair. *Library of Congress*

crowded on the evening of January 3, 1862 as Horace Greeley, the powerful Abolitionist leader, delivered his speech, the first of a series to be given by prominent Americans.

President Lincoln happened to be on the platform. As Greeley, in a frenzy of oratory, proposed the end of slavery as "the one sole purpose of the War," he faced the President, addressing his words directly to him. A public uproar ensued with people standing, cheering and clapping, but Mr. Lincoln sat "with an impassive face."

This event was one of many pressures forcing the President steadily toward resolving the slavery issue. Four months later he signed a bill abolishing slavery in the District of Columbia, and five months after that he issued the Emancipation Proclamation. But it was not until January, 1865, that the Thirteenth Amendment passed, abolishing slavery from United States territory.

In early 1862 an Army officer entered Mr. Lincoln's office with no less than Professor Henry himself as his prisoner. "Mr. President," he announced, "I told you a month ago that Professor Henry is a rebel. Last night at midnight he flashed red lights from the top of his building, signaling to the Secesh. I saw him myself!"

Lincoln looked at the physicist. "Now you're caught! What have you to say, Professor Henry, why sentence of death should not be immediately pronounced upon you?" Then smiling, he patiently explained to the officer that the night before, he himself had been with Professor Henry in the Smithsonian Tower "experimenting with Army signals."

One of the Lincoln conspirators, John Surratt, mentioned in a letter written to his cousin, "There is no news of importance, except the burning of the Smithsonian Institute . . ." In the final months of the Civil War (January 24, 1865) it had burned on a cold winter's day. The upper part of the main building and the towers were destroyed, but the fire was put out before it reached the lower story.

C-2.
The Sixth Street Wharves

Drive south on Seventh Street from Independence Avenue to Maine Avenue. Cross Maine (fourth traffic light from the National Air & Space Museum), go a very short block to Water Street and turn left. Drive slowly along Water Street with the Washington Channel on your right until you reach the turn-around.

The busy Sixth Street Wharves during the Civil War. The house flying the U.S. flag is the Law home, one of Washington's earliest dwellings and now restored.

Library of Congress

It is hard to believe that this quiet area with little shipping was once a busy water terminal for scores of ships that plied back and forth between Washington and the forward bases of the Army in Virginia. It was also the receiving point for much of the human wreckage from the battlefields. Walt Whitman tells about the wounded coming in from "bloody Chancellorsville."

Early May 1862—". . . You ought to see the scene of the wounded arriving at the landing here at the foot of Sixth Street at night. Two boatloads came about half-past seven last night. A little after eight, it rained a long and violent shower. The pale, helpless soldiers had been debarked, and lay around the wharf . . . anywhere. The rain was probably grateful to them; at any rate they were exposed to it. A few torches light up the spectacle.

"All around—on the wharf, on the ground, out on side places—the men are lying on blankets, old quilts, etc., with bloody rags bound 'round heads, arms, and legs. The attendants are few, and at night few outsiders also; only a few hardworked transportation men and drivers. (The wounded are getting to be common, and people grow callous.)

"The men, whatever their condition, lie there and patiently wait til their turn comes to be taken up. Nearby, the ambulances are now arriving in clusters, and one after another is called to back up and take its load. Extreme cases are sent off on stretchers. The men generally make little or no ado, whatever their sufferings. A few groans that cannot be suppressed and occasionally a scream of pain, as they lift a man into an ambulance.

"Today, as I write, hundreds more are expected, and tomorrow and the next day more, and so on for many days. Quite often they arrive at the rate of one thousand a day."

It was a hot, sweltering July 11, 1864. A little after noon, a line of steamers approached the wharves, and began unloading infantrymen in faded blue at the docks stretching from P Street past Sixth and Seventh Streets. As soon as the gangplanks were down, files of veteran soldiers poured ashore. The lean, tanned youths calmly formed ranks, and almost immediately the column headed up dusty Seventh Street. Crowds gathered quickly. They noticed the Greek cross on the men's caps and someone shouted, "It's the old Sixth Corps; the danger is over."

President Lincoln, too anxious to stay at the White House and wait for news, had driven down to the wharves. He watched, munching a piece of hardtack for lunch, as the men of probably Grant's finest corps came ashore. Someone recognized him, and soon they were all cheering him. But it was too tense a moment for anyone to enjoy. All could hear General Early's cannon and the fortress guns of Fort Stevens thundering at

Women making ammunition in a Federal Arsenal during the war. On June 18, 1864 an accidental explosion occurred at the Washington Arsenal, killing twenty three women. It was the city's worst wartime civil disaster. President Lincoln, War Secretary Stanton and other leaders joined the mourners in the funeral procession to Congressional Cemetery two days later, a line of some 150 carriages.

Library of Congress

each other not six miles north of the White House. Could these men arrive in time?

They could and they did arrive just in time to prevent a thin line of makeshift Union troops from buckling under Early's pressure. Rebel skirmishers had driven in the Union outpost line and were about two hundred yards from the Fort, while masses of Confederate infantry had gathered along the Seventh Street Road for an assault. The veterans in faded blue filed into the trenches; by nightfall, arriving Union troops outnumbered Early's 8000 men; the danger was over. Washington had survived her latest brush with disaster.

C-3.
The Washington Arsenal, now Fort McNair

Drive back to Maine Avenue, which as you proceed east becomes M Street; turn right into Fourth Street SW. Turn left at the end of P Street and then quickly right into the main entrance of Fort McNair, formerly the Washington Arsenal.

Execution of four of the Lincoln conspirators, July 7, 1865. The building to the left is the site of the trial. *Martin Luther King Library*

This was the largest Federal arsenal of the Civil War and the nearest shipping point for ordnance and munitions moving by rail and water to the fighting in Virginia. It was a sight to remember! Across most of the flat peninsula stretching between the Potomac and Anacostia rivers were long rows of hundreds of new cannon, freshly painted gun carriages, mortars, wagons, ambulances and carts. Nearby were great stores of artillery ammunition stacked neatly on the ground—shells and round shot, grape, and canister. Inside brick buildings were stored thousands of rifles and pistols and immense quantities of small arms ammunition. "A constant tide," reported *The Evening Star*, "of muskets, rifles and bayonets pour in and out of the spacious armories." Sometimes these armaments moved with urgent speed to some beleaguered place like Harrison's Landing.

When War Secretary Stanton became alarmed on April 27, 1865, by the publicity given to John Wilkes Booth's body at the Navy Yard, he ordered General Lafayette Baker, chief of the War Department Secret Service, to remove the body and bury it secretly. Baker was a man whose name was detested in the city as an embodiment of deceit and betrayal. He removed the body after nightfall from the deck of the ironclad *Montauk*, and took it downstream by small boat to the unused Federal Prison at Arsenal Point. There a shallow grave was dug in the floor of the jailer's quarters. With a doctor and four soldiers present, Booth's body was buried in an unmarked grave. (The spot is about the front yard of Quarters 14 on Second Avenue.)

Two days later, at about 11:00 P.M., the Lincoln conspirators were brought from the Navy Yard to the old Arsenal Prison. On May 9 their trial began on the third floor of the prison's east wing. (This building still stands near the tennis courts, which mark the general outline of part of the old prison yard.)

A fascinated public thronged to watch. Among them, General Custer and his new bride made quite a stir. Shrouded in hoods so they could not see or be seen, the prisoners were heavily manacled and suffering from the unseasonably hot June weather. On June 30, after a long, sensational trial, four were sentenced to death. The others went to prison terms at the American devil's island of the day, the Dry Tortugas, a wretched fever-ridden place off the tip of Florida.

A week later on July 7 the four condemned, including Mrs. Mary Surratt, were hanged, and were immediately buried in the prison yard near the gibbet. In 1869 the bodies were released to the families. Mrs. Surratt was reburied in the Mount Olivet Catholic Cemetery in the northeast quarter of the city.

C-4.
The Navy Yard

Return the way you came to M Street SW, then turn right on M Street and drive to the Navy Yard entrance at M and Eighth Streets SE, somewhat more than a mile. Turn right into the Yard.

President Lincoln enjoyed a visit to the Navy Yard, fascinated by its purposeful bustle and activity. As the closest Federal Naval Station to the blockade, it hummed along at peak capacity. Eighteen hundred skilled workers manned shifts in its copper mill, foundry, carpenter and machine shops. They pounded out the latest naval cannon, gun carriages, anchors, heavy chain cable, ships' boilers, etc.—all the essentials for ships too long on blockade duty in the stormy western Atlantic. Warships whose names, among them the *Monitor*, were famous bywords, dropped anchor here for refit. In late March, 1862, the curious gaped at her dented turret and odd appearance while crew members scrambled ashore, headed for a good time in the city.

When he visited the Army in Virginia, Lincoln generally took a small, fast steamer from the Yard, sometimes the *Carrie Martin* or the *River Queen.* By ship he could get safely down river to the Army's base of operations; the guerrilla infestation of Northern Virginia made it too dangerous to go by rail. The trips were like a vacation to him. "It is a great relief," he once said, "to get away from Washington and the politicians. But nothing touches the tired spot."

The building where the trial was held survives today. Now used for officers' quarters, it can best be seen from Second Avenue in today's Fort McNair.
Susan C. Lee

At the Navy Yard. The body of John Wilkes Booth, Lincoln's assassin, undergoes an autopsy on the deck of the monitor "Montauk," on the afternoon of April 28, 1865. The remains were secreted from the Monitor that evening and taken by small boat to the Washington Arsenal. There they were buried late at night under the ground floor of the jailor's quarters (about the front lawn of Officers' Quarters No. 14).

Junior League of Washington

About nine in the evening, April 9, 1865, the *River Queen* docked at the Navy Yard, back from City Point, Virginia. The Lincoln family debarked, taking their carriage to the White House. As they drove out the main gate, they saw bonfires and crowds of noisy, celebrating people. Tad, the President's small son, called out to a bystander for an explanation. The man replied, "Why, where have you been? Lee has surrendered!"

Late in the afternoon of April 14, 1865, Mr. Lincoln took a drive with Mrs. Lincoln to the Navy Yard. He felt deeply happy because the war was over, and stretched his legs on the deck of the monitor *Montauk* moored at the dock. Two weeks later to the day, the body of his assassin, John Wilkes Booth, lay on a table on the forward deck of this same *Montauk* for autopsy.

C-5.
The Marine Barracks

As you leave the Navy Yard, drive to the north, up Eighth Street SW just past I Street—about three short blocks. The Marine Barracks is to your right and can be given a brief look. Cars parked on the street should be securely locked.

Early in the Republic's history President Jefferson rode his horse into this area one day to pick the site of the Marine Barracks and the Marine Commandant's house. The latter is at the north end of the parade ground and has been used ever since as the home of the serving Commandant of the Corps, a four-star general.

On the early afternoon of a rainy fall day, October 17, 1859, the Marine Barracks was in a state of uproar. Startled marines crowded about putting on their combat gear, drawing muskets, ball cartridges and field rations. The only combat troops in town, they formed up and marched to the Baltimore & Ohio Depot with two howitzers in tow. Eighty-six marines climbed aboard a special train and departed at 3:30 P.M. for Harpers Ferry.

By this time they knew that an insurrection had broken out in the Federal arsenal of this small Potomac River town; a band of armed men had seized the weapons and ammunition there and were attempting to incite a slave uprising.

About 7:00 A.M. the next day the marines, led by Army Colonel Robert E. Lee, charged the arsenal and captured a handful of desperate men headed by the fiery abolitionist zealot, John Brown. The marine contingent quietly returned to the barracks in Washington.

John Brown was hanged in Charlestown, West Virginia, shortly thereafter, but he had loosed the dogs of war. Within two years the South had seceded and the war had well begun. Curiously, only one of the four marine officers present remained with the Union. Of the two army officers also there, the first, Colonel Lee, rose to be the celebrated Confederate commander of the Army of Northern Virginia. The second, J.E.B. Stuart, became General Lee's great cavalry commander.

The United States Marines Barracks in 1861, looking from Eighth Street SE not unlike it does today.   *National Archives*

The rebuilt Long Bridge about 1864 from the Virginia side. The Capitol is in the distance with its completed dome. There were now two spans; the new railroad bridge is seventy-five feet upstream from the original vehicular bridge. Planking has been removed to discourage sudden raids by bands of enemy cavalry.

National Archives

C-6.
The Long Bridge

Drive around the block on which the Marine Barracks are located. Returning to I Street SE, take a right turn and drive west, keeping the Southeast Freeway on your left. Drive six blocks and the road becomes a ramp, taking you up onto the Freeway heading west. Follow the signs for Virginia and you will approach the George Mason Memorial Bridge over the Potomac River. Some exciting things happened about two-tenths of a mile downstream, for this was the site of the Long Bridge, Washington's main bridge to Virginia during the Civil War.

It was just after midnight on May 24, 1861, a clear moonlit night. Virginia had seceded from the Union the day before. Ten thousand Union troops were backed up on the Washington approaches of the Long Bridge and two other bridges leading into Virginia. Most were here. Cavalry dashed across the bridge to clear away Confederate pickets. Then the troops went forward

(deliberately out of step to keep from knocking the bridge down). By morning the Union held all of Arlington Heights, and Alexandria too. The war had begun.

It had happened so easily that Private Winthrop of the Seventh New York lay in the shade the next day and penned a note, "Nothing men can do—except picnics with ladies in straw hats with feathers—is so picturesque as soldiering."

About dawn on July 22, 1861 it was raining, muddy and gloomy. The invasion of Virginia was a dead loss. The Union had been routed the day before near Bull Run Creek. Most of the troops, panic-stricken, had thrown away their rifles and walked all night in a surging, leaderless mob towards Washington. By the time they reached the Long Bridge, there were still some intact units, but what the city saw mostly were thousands of lost, famished boys in filthy uniforms walking in a daze of fatigue toward the safety of the city. Mixed among them were sutler's wagons, congressmen's carriages, artillery caissons, and mounted officers looking for their men. Many lay down in the gutters, sidewalks and doorsteps and went to sleep in the rain. Others begged food, and some hung around saloons. It was a shocking sight, except to southern sympathizers, who didn't bother to hide their joy.

On September 2, 1862, one year had passed since the disaster at Bull Run. It seemed like a repeating bad dream to Washingtonians, but here again were beaten soldiers, dragging themselves across the Long Bridge. Begrimed, weaponless, they gathered tired and discouraged in the city streets. All had heard the cannon and knew the Union had been beaten on the same battlefield of a year ago—Bull Run. People feared that Lee's men would soon appear at the Long Bridge itself.

But this time there were differences. Fewer stragglers were seen, and many solid units were still far forward and fighting hard. Besides, six ungainly, dangerous-looking gunboats had steamed up the Potomac and were anchored around the Aqueduct and Long Bridges, their heavy naval cannon shotted and trained on the Virginia shores. They bore intriguing names like *Aroostook*, *Washusetts*, *Teiga* and *Teaser*. Citizens in the capital were reassured by their business-like appearance.

The single-span Long Bridge had periodically broken down under the load of vehicles, trains and troops that poured back and forth daily between Washington and the war zone. A second wooden and masonry span was completed in mid-1863, seventy-five feet upstream to handle rail traffic only.

The two bridges lasted the rest of the century, and then were replaced in 1906 by two steel-truss bridges. The 1906 rail bridge is still there, but the highway bridge has been replaced since the early 1950's by three modern bridges.

C-7.
Arlington House or The Lee Mansion

To approach Lee Mansion cross the George Mason Bridge into Virginia, turn right at the south end of the bridge and drive west on The George Washington Memorial Parkway. Drive to the traffic circle (one mile plus) at the south end of the Arlington Memorial Bridge. Go left half way around the circle, heading southwest into Memorial Drive. Turn left at the cemetery gate and enter the parking lot. Take the tourmobile to the mansion and the rest of the cemetery tour.

Copied from the Temple of Poseidon at Paestum, this early Greek Revival mansion with Doric columns occupies a striking site on Arlington Heights two hundred feet above the Potomac. From this stately home the

family of Robert E. Lee looked down in early 1861 upon the whole city of Washington.

On April 20, 1861, Mrs. Lee, its owner and the grand-daughter of Martha Washington, had much on her mind. Her husband, Colonel Lee, had resigned that very day from the U.S. Army and would leave soon for Richmond. She hurriedly dashed off a note to her daughter, Mildred, at boarding school. "With a sad and heavy heart, my dear child, I write, for the prospects before us are sad indeed, and I think both parties (North and South) are wrong in this fratricidal War . . ."

On May 16, 1861 Mrs. Lee left Arlington forever. A week later, May 23, Virginia seceded from the Union. That same night a Union force of 10,000 men flooded across the Potomac from Washington, using all the bridges and steamers as well. By dawn they had seized Arlington Heights and Alexandria. General Irvin McDowell, the Union Commander, promptly made Arlington his headquarters, and many priceless things were looted or destroyed by unknown persons. The hills of Arlington were soon white with the tents of Union regiments arriving daily from the North in the first enthusiasm of the war.

Within days several earthen forts began taking shape on or near the estate, for the area was commanding ground. From it an enemy could fire cannon directly into the grounds occupied by the White House and Executive Department buildings. By 1863 the strongest among these earthworks was Fort Whipple, described as "perfect and beautiful" by the army engineers. It is long gone, but its grounds have become Fort Myer, an active Army post today.

In the summer of 1863 a Freedman's Village was taking shape several hundred yards southeast of the mansion. It became the home of 3000 ex-slaves who were brought here from the city. The Freedmen received free food and lodging, wood for cooking and heating, and worked a 12-hour day for a 12-cent daily wage. There was free schooling for the children and it was considered a model village.

On April 11, 1865 a wonderful moment came when a grand illumination was held to commemorate the end of the war. After dark, Arlington House, like all Washington, was lit up brilliantly by candles, bonfires, rockets and colored lights. The Freedmen were there celebrating, too—dancing on the front lawn in a delirium of freedom and release from the war. They sang what was in their hearts:

"De massa run, ha, ha!
De darkey stay, ho, ho!
It mus' be now de kingdum comin',
An' de yar ob jubilo."

The Greek Revival porch of Arlington House looks down upon the Eternal Flame of the Kennedy gravesite in the foreground.

Susan C. Lee

Meanwhile something else was to happen to Arlington that would mean the Lees could never return.

On May 13, 1864 President Lincoln and General Meigs were on a routine visit to the Army's tent hospital near the mansion. They noticed the bodies of twelve soldiers awaiting delivery to the Soldier's Home for burial. Both knew the cemetery was full. Considering the numbers of soldiers dying daily in Washington's hospitals and the shiploads of more wounded coming up the Potomac from Grant's battles in the Wilderness, something had to be done. Looking around him at the open space, General Meigs ordered that the men be buried at Arlington. The first burial was of a Confederate soldier; the remainder, Union men.

By the war's end in 1865, many thousands of soldier dead had been buried at Arlington, hundreds of them unknown. A Civil War veteran, Colonel O'Hare, wrote a poem that tells how his own generation on both sides of the war felt about these soldier dead. Today the words of the first verse seem to echo like a distant bugle call through the long rows of gravestones and across the grassy, tree-filled slopes.

> *"On fame's eternal camping ground,*
> *Their silent tents are spread,*
> *And glory guards with solemn round*
> *The bivouac of the dead."*

Artist's conception of President Lincoln on horseback watching the fighting at Fort Stevens the evening of July 11, 1864. To his left is the fort firing its cannon, to his front the Seventh Street Road (now Georgia Avenue) . . . In mid-distance is the Union picket line probing forward, followed in the near distance by a Union battle line. Beyond the picket line in the trees are burning farm buildings (now the location of Walter Reed Army Medical Complex). At the edge of the trees and stretching far on both sides of Seventh Street is the Confederate battle line. It took one more attack the next evening, July 12, to bring on a Confederate withdrawal.

Junior League of Washington

C-8.
Fort Stevens

From the corner of Pennsylvania Avenue and Seventh Street, drive north on Seventh Street (then Georgia Avenue) for five miles to the crossing of Missouri Avenue (you are following the route of the Union VI Corps to the battle). Go north another two blocks, turn left on Quackenbros Road and look to your right. You will see the rebuilt portion of Fort Stevens, a few of its cannon and a monument marking the spot where President Lincoln watched his first and only battle (Map 13).

It was a little past noon on the sweltering day of July 11, 1864. Jubal Early, commander of the Confederate Second Corps, climbed off his jaded horse and looked south on the Seventh Street Road toward Washington. With his field glasses he could pick out the details of the low earthen fort on the crest of a slope half a mile ahead. He knew it was Fort Stevens, and despite its cannon firing, he recognized signs of weakness and disarray. If he could just get enough men forward to attack quickly, he saw the opportunity of breaking through to capture Washington itself. Such a dazzling stroke, even with the South's chances fading, could perhaps turn the war around. He turned all his energy to the task of hurrying his exhausted men, strung out on the march between Rockville and Silver Spring.

While General Early was hard at work organizing the attack, his chances slipped away. While he watched, long lines of Union troops in faded blue filed into the trenches forward of Fort Stevens. The North had reacted late, but at the eleventh hour General Grant had hurried strong forces from Petersburg to Washington by a fleet of steamers. Their arrival caused General Early some second thoughts. He delayed his attack.

The heat was still oppressive on July 12, 1864, even though a violent thunderstorm had drenched the countryside at about two in the afternoon. The hills behind Fort Stevens were crowded with Washingtonians who had come to watch the battle. About 6:00 it started, as strong Union forces attacked north up the Seventh Street Road. Mr. Lincoln didn't want to miss it either. Leaving his carriage at the Fort Stevens sally port, he hurried to the north parapet and climbed on top. There he stood, oblivious to the "whirring minnie balls," absorbed in the panorama around him. He felt and heard the deafening roar of the fortress cannon close to him, saw the burning farm buildings, and most of all watched the long lines of blue figures ahead, working their way in the dust and smoke of exploding shells toward that infinitely dangerous Confederate battle line.

The kind of Confederate soldiers that General Early led into the northern reaches of the District, hard marching, hard fighting men, lean from living on short rations. Some of them, killed in the battle at Fort Stevens, lie in the churchyard of Grace Church in Silver Spring, where often one finds flowers on their monument.
National Archives

General Wright, Commander of the Sixth Corps, suddenly noticed the President standing fully exposed on the parapet, in great danger. At the same moment an officer standing near Lincoln was shot in the leg and fell backward off the parapet. The General ordered the parapet cleared. No response. He then told the President, "This is no place for you; you must step down at once!" Lincoln was still unmoving. Wright pressed again, "A body of soldiers could remove him!" The lanky figure, holding his stovepipe hat, climbed reluctantly down and sat on an ammunition box. But he kept popping up to see what was going on.

That same evening, on the other side, General Early had just finished talking to his generals. He decided to retreat while he still could. A young staff officer, Major Kyd Douglas, was leaving with orders to pull the troops out that same night. Early called out to him, "Major, we haven't taken Washington, but we've scared Abe Lincoln like hell!" Kyd Douglas paused in the doorway, looking back at his grizzled fire-eating boss, "Yes, General, but this afternoon when the Yankee line moved out against us, I think some other people were scared blue as hell's brimstone." "That's true," growled Early, "but it won't appear in history!"

MAP 14.

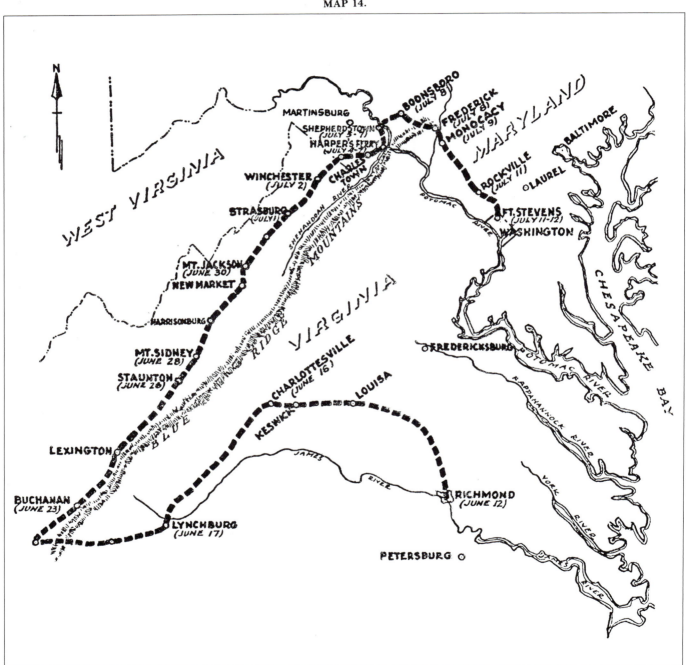

Route of General Early in Raid on Washington, June 12 to July 12, 1864. In one month's time he marched his 10,000 men this enormous distance in blistering hot weather, defeated at least four Federal forces and created near panic in Washington—a brilliant achievement. Map from McClure, *The Defenses of Washington.*

Appendix

MAP 15.

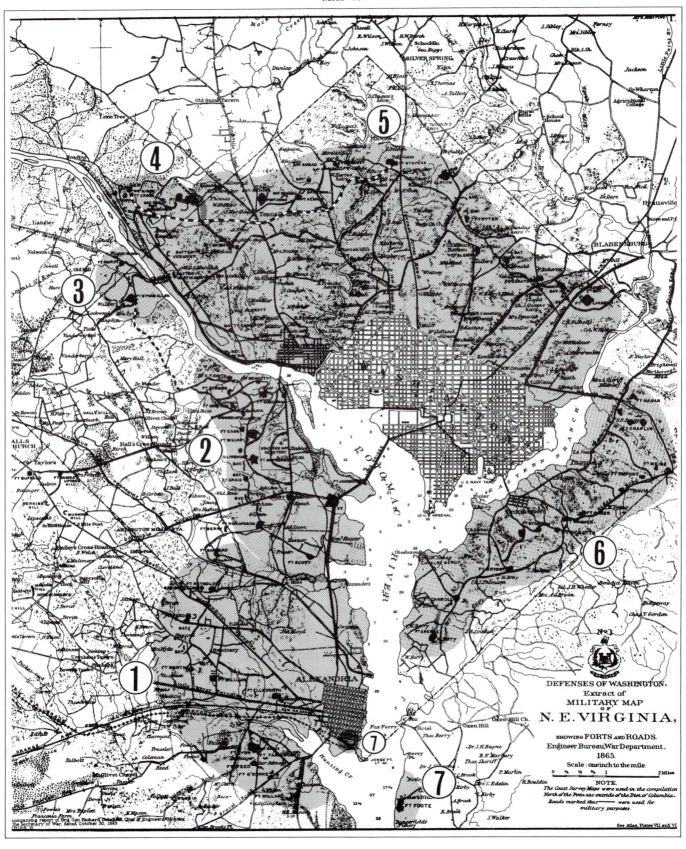

DEFENSES OF WASHINGTON.
Extract of
MILITARY MAP
OF
N. E. VIRGINIA,
SHOWING FORTS AND ROADS.
Engineer Bureau, War Department,
1865.
Scale : one inch to the mile.

NOTE.
The Coast Survey Maps were used in the compilation
North of the Potomac outside the District of Columbia.
Roads marked thus —— were used for
military purposes.

The Suburbs of Washington— A Ring of Forts

Two of Washington's wartime forts have been partially restored, Fort Stevens and Fort Ward. The route to the first is shown on Map 13. Fort Ward is five miles south of the Fourteenth Street bridges on Route 95. Leave Route 95 at the Route 7 exit, turn east on this route crossing over Route 95. Turn right to Fort Ward Park. The City of Alexandria has restored the northwest bastion, and the remaining earthworks of the Fort are almost intact. Around it is a pleasant, wooded park on high, breezy ground suitable for a picnic.

By war's end in 1865, the suburbs of the city would astonish anyone who had last seen the capital before the war. As one left the city to the north he would first see bare, open ground, often swampy and littered with trash, then an area of low foothills filled with camps, barracks, hospitals and training areas. Farther on, two to five miles from the city, he would come to the forts sitting on the tops of Washington's surrounding hills like giant anthills, blocking the roads and valley approaches to the city.

The forts (Map 14) formed a thirty-seven mile circle entirely around Washington. There were sixty-eight of them, mounting over 800 large fortress cannon and spaced about 700 to 1500 yards apart. Between the forts were ninety-three prepared field artillery positions ready for instant occupation. Also, between and forward of the forts were twenty miles of trenches for riflemen. Trees had been felled for about two miles around the forts to provide clear fields of fire.

Most of the forts were not large. One of the larger, Fort Stevens, was perhaps 300 feet wide by 600 feet long and sited seventeen heavy cannon. The walls were twenty to thirty feet thick and constructed of earth

---

Civil War Defenses of Washington – A Circle of Forts.

Area 1 – Forts holding Alexandria.
Area 2 – Forts shielding Arlington Heights, the Long Bridge and Aqueduct Bridge, a direction of great danger.
Area 3 – Forts defending the Chain Bridge above Georgetown.
Area 4 – Forts protecting the city reservoirs.
Area 5 – Forts holding the vulnerable northern approaches.
Area 6 – Forts in the city's safest sector, the southeast.
Area 7 – Two forts with the heaviest cannon and thickest walls of all. These were to block the Potomac River against Confederate warships seeking to attack the city.
Military Roads – Marked by dotted lines, they were used to supply some of the forts. Both are still called "Military Road" and parts of them survive in the city's street system today.

strengthened by logs. Artillery had grown so powerful that the old type of stone and brick walls was too fragile.

Generally in front of the walls was a dry moat or ditch to make it difficult for infantry troops to scale the walls. In front of the moat was an abatis, an early form of "barbed wire" barrier. It consisted of rows of tree limbs and branches stuck into the ground, arranged to impede the advance of infantry soldiers and to trap them under the murderous fire of the defenders.

How did the circle of forts come about? It simply grew in response to a sense of real and present danger. Washington's first Civil War forts were public buildings within the city itself—the Capitol, the Patent Office, the City Hall and the Treasury in the spring of 1861—an emergency arrangement. The few regular troops in the city made these buildings as strong as possible with cannon in the entrance ways and barricades of make-shift design.

Once Federal troops were on the southern shores of the Potomac (May, 1861), a start was made immediately on a few forts in the Arlington-Alexandria area, at least two of the biggest in the wrong places. However, it took the general panic that swept Lincoln's government after

Rifle pits are being dug on Arlington Heights, the labor of tens of thousands of young Bluecoats during the summer, fall and winter of 1861–1862. About twenty miles of these trenches were eventually dug around the city. *Library of Congress*

the First Battle of Bull Run to generate the energies and planning necessary to erect the entire fort system.

Construction was spurred by the good fortune that General McClellan, the Army Commander, was an engineer. Also, the engineer officer directly in charge of construction, General Barnard, possessed the skill, energy and persistence for such a large undertaking. Of course, an enormous aid was the available labor supply in the growing Union Army camped around Washington during that first fall and winter of the war. By March, 1862, forty-six forts of the eventual sixty-eight were completed, a prodigious effort for a period of some ten months.

Priorities in construction were dictated by the directions perceived as the most dangerous. The first forts

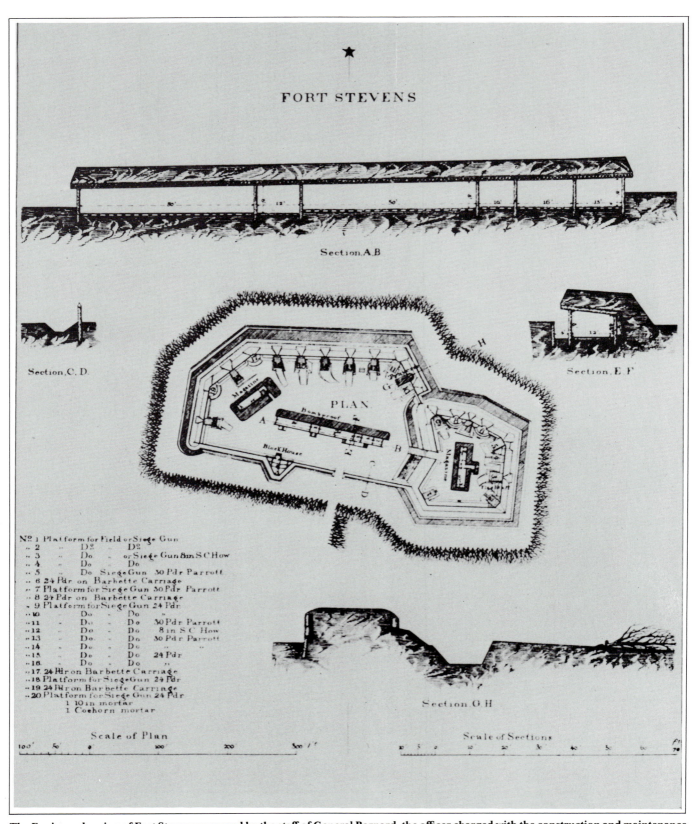

FORT STEVENS

The Engineer drawing of Fort Stevens prepared by the staff of General Barnard, the officer charged with the construction and maintenance of the fort system for most of the war—no small job.

National Archives

Battery Martin Scott, a fortified group of heavy cannon which guarded the Chain Bridge approach to Washington throughout the war.
Martin Luther King Library

rose south of the Potomac to meet a sudden thrust from the west against the hills at Arlington which overlooked the city. Then, planners realized that the city was dangerously vulnerable across its whole northern perimeter to a hostile army crossing the upper Potomac and descending on the city's rear. In spite of a powerful line of seventeen enclosed forts blocking all main roads to the west, north and east, General Barnard later judged that the city was most vulnerable from the north—down the Seventh Street Road. This proved to be the direction of General Early's 1864 thrust which nearly took the city.

About this same time the city's defenders realized that Washington's recently constructed water supply system on the Maryland side of the Potomac, with its holding and distributing reservoirs in the present MacArthur Boulevard area, was vulnerable to seizure. A special group of forts, battery locations and trenches were dug, armed and manned to secure this area.

The forts that completed the perimeter were built on a series of low hills just south of the Anacostia River running southwest to the Potomac River above Alexandria (but on the opposite bank). Once Union gunboats had closed the Potomac to the Confederates (March, 1862), this area was unreachable by the Confederate Army. The forts were built no doubt to protect the Navy Yard, the Federal Arsenal, and the two bridges across the Anacostia River into the city, against sneak raids which were still possible by small hostile forces.

Finally two forts were built with the special task of protecting the city against a possible naval attack up the Potomac River. Battery Rogers was sited just south of Alexandria on a bluff overlooking the river and Fort Foote, a mile downstream on the opposite bank. These had the thickest walls and the heaviest cannon of all, for they were designed to survive the naval guns of enemy ironclad warships.

A highly useful addition to the circle of forts were two

military roads (one on each side of the Potomac) built to provide quick access to certain of the forts for purposes of resupply and quick reinforcement. Fragments of these roads remain today integrated into Washington's road network, known then and now as Military Road. (Map 14)

Once the forts were available, the question of what size garrison was taken up. It was the age-old question that has long plagued military men—How much is enough? President Lincoln and his Cabinet were acutely sensitive to the need for ample, garrison forces for Washington, "the heart of Federal power." At one time early in 1862, the President seemed to favor most of the Army (less 50,000) covering Washington. McClellan's corps commanders favored a 40,000-man garrison plus a maneuver force of another 25,000 operating south of the Potomac. McClellan himself favored a 20,000-man garrison. From these estimates the actual strength of the garrison rose and fell, perhaps a barometer of the proximity to danger felt at different times by the Administration. After the Second Battle of Bull Run (September, 1862) about 70,000 infantry, cavalry and artillery garrisoned the city, probably the lowest point in the Union's fortunes. Then, as the threat eased in the early summer of 1864, with General Grant laying siege to Richmond itself and his Army in need of thousands of replacements, the garrison of the city was drained to its lowest level since early 1861, probably about 10,000 mostly raw troops. This was the time (June–July, 1864), when General Lee, at great risk, shook General Early's Second Corps loose from the defenses of Richmond for the raid that caught the Union by surprise—and nearly captured the city.

Fort Haggerty. In addition to the eastern forts, batteries and trenches, the defense system around the city used a few blockhouses, reminiscent of the Indian country. This wooden blockhouse was sited near the present Key Bridge, across from Roosevelt Island.
National Archives

Drill alternated with endless manual labor to maintain the forts in fighting condition. Washington's heavy summer rains, freezes and thaws in winter, and simply the presence of so many men living and moving about the forts caused rapid deterioration of their earthen construction. Where disciplined units, like some of the heavy artillery regiments, were occupying a fort, unit pride and exacting commanders often kept a fort in splendid condition, but these cases were probably the exception. Hardly were some forts built before they fell into disrepair, were cannibalized by garrisons of other forts seeking lumber and other supplies; then they were discovered by engineer inspectors to be in seriously dilapidated condition. The soldiers hated to work on the forts; some units refused to do so. By early 1863 the great circle of forts had steadily lost ground to the weather and the depredations of soldiers and civilians; General Barnard appealed repeatedly for help from Secretary Stanton. It became necessary to import Irish immigrant labor from as far as New York to restore the forts to an acceptable standard.

The spring of 1864 saw the entire circle of sixty-eight forts probably "at its peak of effectiveness." Then with the end of the war just one year later (April, 1865) all work halted abruptly on the forts, and the Army of the Potomac was hurriedly demobilized by mid-summer. Nine months after hostilities only twelve of Washington's forts were still in commission. Six months later, mid-1866, found only four left. Today Fort Myer (then Fort Whipple) sits on its Civil War site on Arlington Heights, the single active-duty surviving fort of the entire thirty-seven-mile circle of forts. However, the earthen fort itself is long gone.

Once it was hoped to retain the land on which the forts stood and convert them into a circle of parks around the city joined by a scenic drive, but most have now been swallowed by the city. Some sites are still marked by a park, a few by uneven lumps and depressions of earth on private property, but most simply bear a sign indicating that once Fort so-and-so stood nearby.

Was the circle of forts worth the expense, continuing maintenance, and the tying up of so many thousands of men as garrison troops? There are so many "ifs" and "mights" it is hard to decide. However, it seems that the forts possibly deterred General Lee from direct attacks against the city. General Early's advancing army, of course, was halted by the presence of Fort Stevens with its fortress guns blocking the Seventh Street Road. Fort Stevens probably saved the capital in 1864 from a destructive battle in its streets between Early's 8,000 men and the arriving blue-clad soldiers from the Union Sixth and Nineteenth Corps. While the Army of the Potomac was clearly the real barrier between Lee's Army and Washington, the forts added an additional defense that General Lee did not choose to attack with all his forces.

CHRONOLOGY OF CIVIL WAR EVENTS IN AND NEAR WASHINGTON

1861

Feb. 23 — President-elect Lincoln arrives about 6:00 A.M. at the Baltimore & Ohio Depot.

Mar. 4 — President Lincoln's First Inauguration. Capitol and Pennsylvania Avenue under heavy guard.

Apr. 13 — Fort Sumter falls.

Apr. 18 — Francis P. Blair offers the command of the Army to Colonel Robert E. Lee.

Apr. 19 — President Lincoln announces the blockade of the southern states.

Apr. 25 — The Sixth Massachusetts Regiment arrives at Washington's rail depot after fighting a mob in the streets of Baltimore.

Apr. 27 — President Lincoln suspends *writ of habeas corpus* along the military line between Washington and Philadelphia.

Apr.–May — U.S. Capitol, Treasury and other public buildings used as forts, army barracks and supply centers.

May 16 — Mrs. R. E. Lee leaves Arlington House for the last time.

May 23 — Virginia secedes from the Union.

May 24 — Union troops seize Arlington Heights and Alexandria.

May–June — Southern Congressmen and officials depart city to join Confederacy.

June 18 — Professor T.S.C. Lowe makes first aerial flight above Washington in balloon *Enterprise*.

July 2 — Army opens "Soldier's Rest" next to the Baltimore & Ohio Depot.

July 16 — Union forces begin twenty-five-mile march from Washington to Bull Run.

July 21 — Confederate Army defeats Union Army at Bull Run.

July 22 — Defeated Union Army flees into city, a mob.

July 27 — General George B. McClellan takes command of Union forces at Washington.

Aug. 3 — Famous Rebel spy, Mrs. Greenhow, arrested.

Aug. 9 — Mr. Frederick Knapp, Sanitary Commission, begins his help to needy soldiers in the city.

Aug. 24 — Washington's Mayor Berret arrested for disloyalty, imprisoned at Fort Lafayette, New York.

Oct. 21 — Union forces defeated at Ball's Bluff near Leesburg, Va.

Nov. 1 — General Winfield Scott retires as Army general-in-chief, replaced by General McClellan.

Nov. 8 — Confederate envoys to Britain and France seized on British ship *Trent*.

Nov. 19 — Julia Ward Howe writes the *Battle Hymn of the Republic* in the early morning at Willard's Hotel.

Dec. 26 — Serious fire at horse and mule corrals, Camp Fuller (site of present State Department).

Winter of 1861–62 — Large Union Army, building to 200,000 men, camps near Washington, prepares for battle and builds a circle of forts around the city.

1862

Mar. 9 — Ironclad warships *Monitor* and *Merrimac* fight to a draw at Hampton Roads, Virginia.

— Confederates abandon Bull Run defense position, also batteries along west shore of Potomac below city, and move south.

Mar. 17 — Army of Potomac begins embarking from Washington and Alexandria ports, bound for Virginia Peninsula and advance on Richmond.

Apr. 5 — Peninsular campaign opens.

Apr. 16 — Act of Congress ends slavery in the District of Columbia.

May 23
June 9 — Stonewall Jackson begins whirlwind campaign in Valley of Virginia, threatens Washington gravely.

June 1 — McClellan's army near Richmond fights Battle of Fair Oaks. Numbers of wounded and sick arrive Washington daily by boat.

June 2 — Hard-fought local election held in D.C. Mayor Wallach, incumbent Republican, wins.

July 2 — After seven days of battle, General McClellan's army is driven into a bridgehead at Harrison's Landing. Surge of wounded and sick coming into Washington.

July 11 — General Halleck appointed general-in-chief of Army. Stays at Washington headquarters (Winder Building).

Aug. 2 — Washington's first horsecars begin running from the Capitol to the Treasury.

Aug. 16 — General McClellan's army begins withdrawal by water back to Alexandria to cover capital as General Lee swings north.

Aug. 28-30 — Second Battle of Bull Run, a heavy defeat for the Union.

Sep. 1 — Union forces barely block Stonewall Jackson's flank attack on retreating Union forces near Chantilly.

Sep. 2 — President Lincoln gives command of the retreating army to General McClellan.

Sep. 2 — Federal gunboats brought upriver to protect the Potomac bridges and Virginia shoreline against a Confederate breakthrough.

Sep. 5 — Gen. Lee's army turns away from Washington and invades Maryland, seizing Frederick.

Sep. 6 — Under General McClellan the Army of the Potomac marches north through Washington and Rockville, Maryland in pursuit of Lee's Army.

Sep. 14 — Union forces drive part of Lee's army from South Mountain west of Frederick.

— Clara Barton leaves Washington in an army wagon bound for the fighting.

Sep. 17 — General McClellan wins battle against Lee at Antietam Creek near Sharpsburg, Maryland, the first important victory for the Union in the east.

Sep. 22 — President Lincoln issues the preliminary Emancipation Proclamation.

Sep. 24 — President Lincoln suspends *writ of habeas corpus* for all persons arrested by military authority.

Nov. 5 — Lincoln removes General McClellan from command. General Burnside takes his place.

Dec. 13 — Army of the Potomac under General Burnside heavily defeated at Battle of Fredericksburg, Virginia.

Dec. 31 — West Virginia admitted as 35th State of Union.

1863

Jan. 1 — Emancipation Proclamation takes effect.

Jan. 25 — General Hooker supercedes General Burnside as commander of the Army of the Potomac.

May 4 — General Lee's Army again defeats the Army of the Potomac with great losses at Chancellorsville, Virginia.

June 3 — Lee's army begins invasion of the North.

July 3 — Army of the Potomac under a new commander, General Meade, defeats Lee's Army at Gettysburg after three days of battle.

July 4 — Citizens of Washington celebrate news of the victory at Gettysburg.

July 5 — City learns of General Grant's victory at Vicksburg.

July 13 — Lee's Army escapes back across the Potomac into Virginia.

Sep. 15 — President Lincoln suspends *writ of habeas corpus* throughout the Union.

Nov. 26 — First national observance of Thanksgiving throughout the Union.

Dec. 4 — Potomac River water, flowing through pipes in aqueduct from Great Falls, arrives in city for first time.

1864

Mar. 12 — Lt. General Grant named general-in-chief of Union Army.

May 5–8 — Great battle occurs between the armies of Lee and Grant in the Virginia Wilderness. Grant moves south.

May 8–19 — Armies collide again in another large battle near Spotsylvania Court House.

May 7–30 — Washington and other eastern cities filling with sick and wounded.

May 13 — General Meigs and President Lincoln decide to use the Arlington Estate as a Federal cemetery.

May 16 — Union Army of the James suspends attacks on Richmond and bottles itself up at Burmuda Hundred.

June 3 — Lee's and Grant's armies again fight at Cold Harbor, Grant fails to break through with large losses.

June 7 — Republican Convention nominates Lincoln for a second term.

June 12–18 — Grant's Army sideslips to the east of Richmond, moves south of the James River and fails to capture Petersburg, a major rail center of Richmond.

June 28 — Congress repeals the Fugitive Slave Law.

May–June — Washington area hospitals are crowded with wounded and sick men. From May 5 to June 15, General Grant's Army has lost over 38,000 wounded. This does not count heavy losses in killed and missing.

July 2 — General Early, leading Confederate II Corps, has defeated one Union force after another, now controls Valley of Virginia.

July 4 — Lincoln pockets radical reconstruction bill passed by Congress.

July 9 — General Early defeats Union force at Monocacy River, just southeast of Frederick, Maryland.

— Refugee wagons fleeing from Early's troops begin entering city on Rockville Pike (Wisconsin Avenue) and Seventh Street Road (Georgia Avenue). Some panic in the city.

July 11 — General Early's troops enter D.C. from north on the Seventh Street Road about mid-day, are halted at Fort Stevens.

— Parts of Union VI and XIX corps, sent by Grant, start landing at the Sixth Street Wharves about the same time.

July 12 — Skirmishing continues all day. Union VI Corps troops launch evening attack.

— General Early's army retreats after darkness falls, escapes a day later across the Potomac near Leesburg.

Sep. 2 — Atlanta falls to General Sherman's Army.

Sep. 22 — General Sheridan defeats Early's Army near Winchester, Virginia.

Oct. 19 — General Early's Army mostly destroyed by much larger Union Army under Sheridan near Cedar Creek, Virginia.

Nov. 8 — Election Day—Lincoln reelected President.

Nov. 15 — General Sherman's Army leaves Atlanta—starts march through Georgia.

Dec. 21 — General Sherman captures Savannah, Georgia.

1865

Jan. 15 — Fort Fisher, Confederate's last open port falls.

Jan. 24 — Smithsonian castle suffers damage from severe fire.

Jan. 31 — The Thirteenth Amendment abolishing slavery passes Congress.

Feb. 1 — Sherman's Army starts north into the Carolinas.

Feb. 3 — Peace Conference between Lincoln and Confederate Commissioners held on *River Queen* in Hampton Roads.

Mar. 3 — Freedmen's Bureau enacted by Congress to provide care for blacks.

Mar. 4 – President Lincoln's Second Inauguration.

Mar. 5 – Lincoln's inaugural ball held at Patent Office.

Apr. 2 – General Grant breaks through Confederate line at Petersburg.

Apr. 3 – Richmond falls. President Davis flees.

Apr. 9 – General Lee surrenders his Army at Appomattox Court House. In Washington impromptu celebration starts.

Apr. 11 – Grand victory celebration and illumination held in Washington.

Apr. 14 – President Lincoln shot at Ford's Theater. Assassin John Wilkes Booth escapes into southern Maryland.
– Lewis Payne stabs Secretary Seward in his home same evening.

Apr. 15 – President Lincoln dies in early morning at the Petersen House across the street from the Theater.
– Vice President Andrew Johnson sworn in as President.

Apr. 17 – Mrs. Mary Surratt arrested as conspirator at her boardinghouse on H Street.

Apr. 19 – Funeral of President Lincoln held in East Room of White House.
– Lincoln's remains taken to Capitol in great parade along crowded Pennsylvania Avenue.

Apr. 21 – Lincoln's funeral train leaves Washington.

Apr. 26 – John Wilkes Booth, the assassin of Lincoln, is shot to death in a barn near Port Royal, Virginia.
– General Joseph E. Johnson negotiates surrender terms with General Sherman near Raleigh, North Carolina.

May 10 – Trial of Lincoln conspirators begins in Federal Prison at U.S. Arsenal, Washington. Ends June 30.

May 22 – The Lincoln family leaves Washington.

May 23–24 – Grand Review of Meade's and Sherman's Armies on Pennsylvania Avenue before President Johnson.

July 7 – Four of the Lincoln conspirators, including Mrs. Surratt, hanged.

Nov. 10 – Captain Henry Wirz, Confederate commandant of Andersonville Prison hanged at the Old Capitol Prison.

BIBLIOGRAPHY

Abbott, Asa T. "Second Lieutenant at Fort Stevens." *Civil War Times Illustrated.* Gettysburg: Historical Times, Inc., 1978.

Adams, George W. *Doctors in Blue.* New York: Henry Schuman, 1952.

Adler, William. *Washington—A Reader.* New York: Meredith Press, 1967.

Alexander, Edwin P. *Civil War Railroads and Models.* New York: Clarkson N. Potter, 1977.

Ames, Mary Clemner. *Life and Scenes in the National Capital.* Hartford: A. D. Worthington and Co., 1874.

Architect of the Capitol, *Art in the United States Capitol.* Washington: U.S. Govt. Printing Office, 1978.

Austin, Anne L. *The Woolsey Sisters of New York, 1860–1900.* Philadelphia: American Philosophical Society, 1971.

Bacon-Foster, Cora. "Clara Barton Humanitarian." *Columbia Historical Society Records,* Washington, Vol. 21, 1918.

Balsiger, David, and Sellier, Charles E. *The Lincoln Conspiracy.* Los Angeles: Shick Sunn Classic Books, 1977.

Barnard, J.D. Brevet Maj. Gen., *A Report on the Defenses of Washington.* Washington: U.S. Govt. Printing Office, 1871.

Basler, Roy P. *Abraham Lincoln: His Speeches and Writings.* New York: World Publishing Co., 1946.

Benjamin, Marcus, ed. *Washington During War Time.* Washington: Thirty-Sixth Annual Encampment of the GAR, 1902.

Biddle, James. "Decatur House—Focal Point for a Century and a Half." *Twenty-Fourth Annual Washington Antiques Show.* Washington, 1979.

Billings, Elden E. "Military Activities in Washington in 1861." *Columbia Historical Society Records,* Washington, Vol. 60–62, 1963.

_____. "Social and Economic Conditions in Washington During the Civil War." *Ibid.,* Vol. 1963–1965, 1966.

Bishop, Jim. *The Day Lincoln was Shot.* New York: Harper and Bros., 1955.

Blair, Gist. "Annals of Silver Spring." *Columbia Historical Society Records,* Washington, Vol. 21, 1918.

Blanding, Stephen F. *In the Defense of Washington.* Providence: E. C. Freeman and Son, 1879.

Bowers, Claude G. *The Tragic Era.* Cambridge: The Literary Guild of America, 1929.

Brinton, John. *Personal Memoirs.* New York: Neale Publishing Co., 1914.

Brooks, Noah. *Washington During Lincoln's Time.* New York: Reinhart and Co., 1958.

Brooks, Stewart. *Civil War Medicine.* Springfield: Charles C. Thomas, 1966.

Cable, Mary. *Avenue of the Presidents.* Boston: Houghton Mifflin Co., 1969.

Cammerer, Paul H. *A Manual on the Origin and Development of Washington.* Washington: U.S. Govt. Printing Office, 1939.

Carr, Roland T. *Thirty-Two President's Square.* Washington: Acropolis Books, 1980.

Catton, Bruce. *Mr. Lincoln's Army.* Garden City: Doubleday and Co., 1955.

_____. *This Hallowed Ground. Ibid.,* 1956.

_____. *The Coming Fury. Ibid.,* 1961.

_____. *Prefaces to History. Ibid.,* 1970.

Chase, Enoch A. "The Arlington Case." *Columbia Historical Society Records,* Washington, Vol. 31–32, 1930.

Clark, Allan C. "The Mayors of the Corporation of Washington—Thomas E. Carberry." *Ibid.,* Vol. 19, 1916.

_____. "Richard Wallach and the Times of his Mayoralty." *Ibid.,* Vol. 21, 1918.

_____. "Abraham Lincoln and the National Capital." *Ibid.,* Vol. 27, 1925.

Cobb, Josephine. "M. B. Brady's Photographic Studio in Washington." *Ibid.,* Vol. 53–56, 1959.

Collins, Herbert R. "The White House Stables and Garages." *Ibid.,* Vol. 1963–1965, 1966.

Collis, Septima M. *A Woman's War Record, 1861–1865.* New York: G. P. Putnam and Sons, 1889.

Committee to Preserve Rhodes Tavern. *Pamphlet.* Washington, 1979.

Conger, Clement E. "The White House." *Twenty-Fourth Annual Washington Antiques Show.* Washington, 1979.

Cooling, Benjamin Franklin. *Symbol, Sword and Shield—Defending Washington During the Civil War.* Hamden, Conn.: Archon Books, 1975.

Cox, Warren J. *A Guide to the Architecture of Washington, D.C.* New York: McGraw Hill Book Co., 1974.

—, William V. "The Defenses of Washington—General Early's Advance on the Capital and the Battle of Fort Stevens." *Columbia Historical Society Records.* Washington, Vol. 4, 1901.

Current, Richard N. *The Lincoln Nobody Knows.* New York: McGraw Hill Book Co., 1958.

Curry, Mary E. "The Theodore Roosevelt Island—A Broken Link in Washington, D.C. History." *Columbia Historical Society Records,* Washington, Vol. 1971–1972, 1973.

Crane, Stephen. *The Red Badge of Courage and Selected Stories.* New York: Alfred Knopf, 1960.

Dahomel, James. "Analostin Island" *Columbia Historical Society Records.* Washington, Vol. 35–36, 1935.

Dalzell, James M. "Reminiscences." *Ibid.,* Vol. 27, 1925.

Dannett, Silvia G. L., ed. *Noble Women of the North.* New York: Thomas Yoseloff, 1959.

Davis, Burke. *Our Incredible Civil War.* New York: Ballantine Books, 1960.

—, Harriet Riddle. "Civil War Recollections of a Little Yankee." *Columbia Historical Society Records.* Washington, Vol. 44–45, 1944.

—, Henry E. "Ninth Street and Thereabouts." *Ibid.,* Washington, Vol. 5, 1902.

De Chambrun, Adolphe. *Impressions of Lincoln and the Civil War.* New York: Random House, 1952.

Donald, David H. *Gone For a Soldier.* Boston: Little Brown and Co., 1975.

Douglas, Henry Kyd. *I Rode with Stonewall.* Chapel Hill: U. of N. Carolina Press, 1940.

Edgington, Frank E. *A History of the New York Avenue Presbyterian Church.* Washington, 1961.

Ellis, Dr. John B. *The Sights and Sounds of the Nation's Capital.* New York: Junkin and Co., 1869.

Emery, Fred A. "Washington's Newspapers." *Columbia Historical Society Records.* Washington, Vol. 37–38, 1937.

————. "Washington's Historic Bridges." *Ibid.,* Vol. 30, 1938.

Encyclopaedia Britannica. Chicago: Encyclopaedia Britannica, Inc., 1942.

Enyart, Byron K. *A Mile of Glory.* New York: Vantage Press, 1976.

Ewing, Charles. *Yesterday's Washington, D.C.* Miami: E. S. Seaman Publisher, 1976.

Federal Writer's Project. *Washington City and Capital.* American Guide Series (WPA). Washington: U.S. Govt. Printing Office, 1937.

Fishback, Frederick L. "Washington City, Its Founding and Development." *Columbia Historical Society Records.* Washington, Vol. 20, 1917.

Fishwick, Marshal W. *Illustrious Americans: Clara Barton.* Morristown: Silver Burdett Co., 1966.

Fowler, Robert H. *Album Illustrating the Assassination of Abraham Lincoln.* Gettysburg: Historical Times, Inc., 1965.

Fradin, Morris. *The Story of Clara Barton, Follow the Cannon.* Cabin John, Md.: See and Know Press, 1967.

Freeman, Douglas Southall. *R. E. Lee.* New York: Charles Scribner Sons, 4 vols., 1947.

Froncek, Thomas, ed. *The City of Washington.* Junior League of Washington, New York: Alfred A. Knopf, 1977.

Frye, Virginia K. "St. Patrick's: First Catholic Church of the Federal City." *Columbia Historical Society Records.* Washington, Vol. 23, 1920.

Franklin, John Hope. *The Emancipation Proclamation.* New York: Doubleday and Co., 1963.

Fuller, Maj. General J.F.C., *The Generalship of Ulysses S. Grant.* Bloomington: Indiana University Press, 1929.

GAR Committee. *Catalogue of Points of Historic Interest.* Washington: Thirty-sixth National Encampment, 1902.

Gardner, Alexander. *Gardner's Photographic Sketchbook of the Civil War.* New York: Dover Publications, Inc., 1959.

Goode, James M. *The Outdoor Sculpture of Washington, D.C.* Washington: The Smithsonian Institution, 1974.

————. "Lost Houses on Lafayette Square." *Twenty-Fourth Annual Washington Antiques Show.* Washington, 1979.

Green, Constance M. *The Secret City—A History of Race Relations in the Nation's Capital.* Princeton: Princeton University Press, 1967.

————. *Washington Village and Capital, 1800–1878. Ibid.,* 1962.

————. *The Church on Lafayette Square—A History of St. John's Church.* Washington: Potomac Books, 1970.

Grover, Leonard. "Lincoln's Interest in the Theater." *Century Magazine.* New York: The Century Co., April, 1909.

Guernsey, Albert H. and Alden, Henry M. ed., *Harper's Pictorial History of the Civil War.* New York: The Fairfax Press, 1966.

Harkness, Robert H. "The Old Glass House." *Columbia Historical Society Records.* Washington, Vol. 18, 1915.

Hecht, Arthur. "Marching Up Georgia—A Tour Up Georgia Avenue." *Columbia Historical Society Records.* Washington, Vol. 1963–1965, 1966.

Hibben, Henry B. *Navy Yard Washington.* Washington: U.S. Govt. Printing Office, 1890.

Hibbs, David R. P. *Letters Re Washington, D.C. and the Peninsula Campaign.* Nov. 23, 1861 to April 1, 1862 (unpublished).

Hutchinson's Washington and Georgetown Directory. Washington: Hutchinson and Bros., 1863.

Jensen, Amy L. *The White House and its Thirty-Five Families.* New York: McGraw Hill, 1970.

Johnson, E. H. "Reminiscences of Honorable Edwin M. Stanton, Secretary of War." *Columbia Historical Society Records.* Washington, Vol. 13, 1910.

Johnson, Robt. U. and Buel, Clarence C., ed.. *Battles and Leaders of the Civil War,* New York: The Century Co, 4 vols., 1887.

Jones, Katherine M. *Heroines of Dixie.* New York: Bobbs-Merrill Co., 1955.

—, Virgil Carrington. *Gray Ghosts and Rebel Raiders.* New York: Henry Holt and Co., 1956.

Josephson, Matthew. *The Robber Barons, 1861–1901.* New York: Harcourt Brace and Co., 1934.

Kelly, Dr. Joseph T. "Memories of a Lifetime in Washington." *Columbia Historical Society Records.* Washington, Vol. 31–32, 1930.

Ketchum, Richard N., ed. *The American Heritage Picture History of the Civil War.* New York: Doubleday and Co., 1960.

Kimmel, Stanley P. *The Mad Booths of Maryland.* New York: Bobbs-Merrill Co., 1940.

————. *Mr. Lincoln's Washington.* New York: Coward-McCann, Inc., 1957.

Komer, Frank. *The History of Harvey's.* Washington: Published by Harvey's Restaurant, 1934.

Leech, Margaret. *Reveille in Washington.* New York: Harper and Bros., 1941.

Leslie, Frank. *Illustrated History of the Civil War.* New York: Fairfax Press, 1967.

Lewis, David L. *District of Columbia.* New York: Norton, 1976.

—, Lloyd. *Myths After Lincoln.* New York: Press of the Readers Club, 1929.

————. *Sherman Fighting Prophet.* New York: Harcourt Brace and Co., 1932.

Lowenfels, Walter. *Walt Whitman's Civil War.* New York: Alfred A. Knopf, 1960.

McCardle, Walter F. "The Development of the Business Sector in Washington." *Columbia Historical Society Records.* Washington, Vol. 1973–1974, 1976.

McClellan, H. B. *I Rode with Jeb Stuart.* Bloomington: Indiana Press, 1958.

McClure, Stanley W. *The Defenses of Washington.* Na. Capital Parks, Dept. of Interior. Washington: U.S. Govt. Printing Office, 1957.

McPherson, James M. *The Negro's Civil War.* New York: Pantheon Books, 1965.

Maddox, Diane. *Historic Buildings of Washington, D.C.* Pittsburg: Ober Park Assn. Inc., 1973.

Meredith, Roy. *The World of Matthew Brady.* Los Angeles: Brook House, 1976.

Milder, Keith E. "Angel of Mercy in Washington: Josephine Griffing and the Freedmen, 1864–1872." *Columbia Historical Society Records.* Washington, Vol. 1963–1964, 1964.

Miller, David T. *The Defenses of Washington During the Civil War.* Buffalo: Mr. Copy, Inc., 1976.

—, Francis T., ed. *The Photographic History of the Civil War.* New York: Castle Books, 10 Vols., 1957.

Mitchell, Mary O. "An Intimate Journey Through Georgetown." *Columbia Historical Society Records,* Washington, Vol. 1960–1962, 1963.

Mogelever, Jacob. *Death to Traitors, The Story of General Lafayette C. Baker.* Garden City: Doubleday and Co., 1960.

Moore, Charles. *Washington Past and Present.* New York: The Century Co., 1929.

Mulbridge, Donald H. "The Sanitary Commission in Washington, 1861–1865." *Columbia Historical Society Records.* Washington, Vol. 1960–1962, 1963.

Nolan, John. "Some Aspects of Washington's Nineteenth Development." *Ibid.,* Vol. 1973–1974, 1976.

Nolty, Bernard C. *U.S. Marines at Harpers Ferry and in the Civil War.* Washington: Historical Branch, G-3 Div., Hq. U.S. Marine Corps, 1966.

Ogburn, Charlton. "Birth and Growth of a World Capital." *Holiday Magazine.* Philadelphia: April, 1962.

Olazewski, George J. *Restoration of Ford's Theater.* U.S. National Park Service. Washington: U.S. Govt. Printing Office, 1963.

————. *House Where Lincoln Died. Ibid.,* 1967.

Paullin, Charles O. "Alexandria County in 1861." *Columbia Historical Society Records.* Washington, Vol. 28, 1926.

————. "History of the Site of the Congressional and Folger Libraries." *Ibid.,* Vol. 1937–1938, 1938.

Peck, Taylor. *Round Shot to Rockets.* Annapolis: U.S. Naval Institute, 1949.

Pierce, Lt. Comdr. R. K. *Riverine Warfare.* Navy Department. Washington: U.S. Govt. Printing Office, 1949.

Reid, Robert. *Old Washington, D.C.—In Early Photographs, 1846–1932.* New York: Dover Publications, Inc., 1980.

Reiff, David D. *Washington Architecture 1791–1861.* U.S. Commission of Fine Arts. Washington: U.S. Govt. Printing Office, 1971.

Riddle, Albert G. *Recollections of War Times, 1860–1865.* New York: G. P. Putnam's Sons, 1895.

Robertson, Niente Ingersol. "William Henry Seward" *Twenty-Fourth Annual Washington Antiques Show.* Washington, 1979.

Sandburg, Carl. *Abraham Lincoln, The War Years.* New York: Harcourt Brace and Co., 4 Vols., 1939.

————. *Abraham Lincoln, The Prairie Years and the War Years. Ibid.,* 1954.

Sedgwick, Paul J. *The Shield and Symbol and the Sword.* Washington: D.C. Civil War Centennial Commission, 1965.

Shackelton, Robert. *The Book of Washington.* Philadelphia: Pen Publishing Co., 1922.

Shepherd, Julia A.. "Lincoln's Assassination." *Century Magazine.* New York: The Century Co., April, 1909.

Shipley, Ruth B. "The Historic Winder Building." *Columbia Historical Society Records.* Washington, Vol. 50, 1952.

Shoemaker, Louis P. "Historic Rock Creek." *Ibid.,* Vol. 12, 1909.

Shrdlu,. *An Affectionate Chronicle.* Washington: The National Press Club, 1958.

Simons, Marietta Hennessey. *Letter to Mrs. Janette Harris.* Washington, 1920's (unpublished).

Slanson, Allan B., ed. *A History of the City of Washington—Its Men and Institutions.* Washington: The Washington Post, 1903.

Smith, Hal H. "Historic Washington Homes." *Columbia Historical Society Records.* Washington, Vol. 11, 1908.

Snell, T. Loftin. *The Stranger's Guide to Washington, D.C.* (with Map of Civil War City). Washington: Published by author, 1967.

Spratt, Zack. "Rock Creek Bridges." *Columbia Historical Society Records.* Washington, Vol. 53–56, 1959.

Stark, Hon. Fortney H. "Rhodes Tavern and Washington's Local Roots." *Congressional Record.* Washington: U.S. Govt. Printing Office, May 23, 1979, PE 2487.

Stearns, Amanda. *The Lady Nurse of Ward E.* New York: Baker and Taylor Co., 1909.

Stepp, John W., and Hill, William I., ed. *Mirror of War.* Englewood Cliffs: Prentiss Hall, 1961.

Stevenson, Elizabeth. "Olmstead on F Street—The Beginnings of the Sanitary Commission." *Columbia Historical Society Records.* Washington, Vol. 1973–1974, 1976.

Templeman, Eleanor Lee. *Blair-Lee House, Guest House of the President.* McLean, Va: EPM Publications, Inc., 1980. *Twenty-Fourth Annual Washington Antiques Show.* Washington, 1979.

The Evening Star. Washington, 1861–1865.

Thomas, Katherine E. "The Long Lost Washington Drawing by Major L'Enfant and the Historic McKean House." *Columbia Historical Society Records.* Washington, Vol. 39, 1938.

Topham, Washington. "Central Market and Vicinity." *Ibid.,* Vol. 26, 1924.

————. "First Railroad into Washington." *Ibid.,* Vol. 27, 1925.

————. "The Winder Building." *Ibid.,* Vol. 37–38, 1938.

U. S. Army. *Military Department of Washington, Provost Marshal Records.* Period of Civil War. Record Group 393, U.S. National Archives, Washington.

U. S. Army. *Surgeon General Lists of Washington, Georgetown and Alexandria Army Hospitals.* Period of Civil War. Record Group 94, U.S. National Archives, Washington.

Vandiver, Frank E. *Jubal's Raid.* New York: McGraw Hill Book Co., 1960.

Van Devanter, Ann. "Lafayette Park—Forecourt to the White House." *Twenty-Fourth Annual Washington Antiques Show.* Washington, 1979.

Warner, Brainard H. "1863 Letter." *Columbia Historical Society Records.* Washington, Vol. 31–32, 1930.

Webber, Lt. Richard H. *Monitors of the U.S. Navy, 1861–1937.* Navy Department. Washington: U.S. Govt. Printing Office, 1967.

Weichmann, Louis J. *A True History of the Assassination of Abraham Lincoln and of the Conspiracy of 1865.* New York: Alfred A. Knopf, 1975.

Welles, Gideon. *Diary.* New York: Houghton Mifflin Co., 3 vols., 1911.

Whyte, James H. "Divided Loyalties in Washington During the Civil War." *Columbia Historical Society Records.* Washington, Vol. 1960–1962, 1963.

Wiley, Bill Irwin. *The Life of Billy Yank.* New York: Dobbs Merrill Co., 1951.

Williams, T. Harry. *Lincoln and His Generals.* New York: Alfred A. Knopf, 1952.

Williamson, James J. *Prison Life in the Old Capitol.* West Orange, N.J., 1911.

Wills, Mary Alice. *The Confederate Blockade of Washington, D.C., 1861–1862.* Parsons, W. Va.: McClain Printing Co., 1975.

Wilson, John M. *Defenses of Washington, 1861–1865.* Military

Order of the Loyal Legion of the U.S. Washington: D.C. Commandry, Dec. 4, 1907.

Woodward, Fred E. "A Ramble Among the Boundary Stones of the District of Columbia with a Camera." *Columbia Historical Society Records.* Washington, Vol. 10, 1907.

Worthington, Glen H. *Fighting for Time.* Frederick, Md.: Frederick County Historical Society. 1932.

Young, Agatha B. *The Women and the Crisis.* New York: McDowell, Obolensky Co., 1959.

ACKNOWLEDGMENTS

A number of people possessed special knowledge and skills which they shared with me in the preparation of this book. Among them my particular thanks are due to:

Mr. Michael P. Musick, Archivist, Navy and Old Army Branch, National Archives; Mr. James M. Goode, author and curator of the Smithsonian Institution; Mr. George Stansfield, Librarian of the National War College; Mrs. Roxanna Deane, Supervisor of the Washington Division, Martin Luther King Library, and Mr. G. R. Key, Readers' Advisor of the same Library. Equally, my appreciation is due to Miss Elizabeth Miller, Librarian of the Columbia Historical Society; Miss Diane Maddex, author and Director of Planning of the Preservation Press, National Trust for Historic Preservation; Ms. T. Loftin of the National Geographic Society and Mrs. Severine L. Langelan, Administrative Librarian, Post and Patients Library, Walter Reed Army Medical Center.

In my search for and selection of prints and photographs to illustrate the text my gratitude for a great deal of assistance goes to:

Mr. Leroy Bellamy, Prints and Photographs Division, Library of Congress; Mr. Jonathan Heller, Still Pictures Branch, National Archives; Mrs. Frances Turgeon, Curator of the Kiplinger Print Collection; Miss Anne Imelda Radice, Curator for the Architect of the Capitol; and Miss Gail Mishkin, the Dimmock Gallery of George Washington University. Of special help is the loan of a number of rare prints by Mrs. Douglas Woods Sprunt of the Junior League of Washington.

My research for maps for use with the text was very greatly helped by the staffs of the Map Division, Library of Congress, and graphics offices of the National Park Service and the National Capital Planning Commission. In this respect revisions to the maps required artistic and drafting skills of a high order. These were capably provided by my friend, Mr. John Ozimina, who executed especially pleasing maps for publication.

Mr. Stanley Field, author and mentor, and Mrs. Evelyn Metzger, publisher of EPM Publications, were both of valuable help throughout the writing, editing and publication process by making available to me their experience, positive ideas and many good suggestions.

Much credit and my lasting thanks goes to Susan Lee, my daughter, who in the midst of her own busy career in photography, took time to make a number of splendid photographs of historical buildings in Washington, most of which are included in this book. She also worked with numerous negatives of old prints and photographs, creating fine, clear photographs suitable for publication.

The task of typing two successive drafts of the text fell to my neighbor, Bernice Goodier. Both she and her husband, Arthur Goodier, are responsible for the incorporation of many helpful ideas in the text.

The close interest, patience and staunch support of my mother, Mrs. William E. Lee, was a continuing, necessary encouragement. Finally, the active imagination, flexible approaches to the situations described in the book, and sheer writing ability of my wife, Helen, helped me immeasurably as the work proceeded.

R. M. L.
January 31,
1981